SOMERSET COUNTY
Naturally

A Guide to Enjoying the Wildlife of Somerset County, Pennsylvania

Scott F. Bastian, D.V.M.

2002

Somerset County Naturally: A Guide to Enjoying the Wildlife of Somerset County, Pennsylvania

Copyright © 2002 by Scott F. Bastian

First printing.

ISBN 0-9720594-0-7

Color plates produced by University Lithoprinters, Ann Arbor, Michigan.

Printed in the United States of America by Thomson-Shore, Inc., Dexter, Michigan.

Table of Contents

4

Pennsylvania

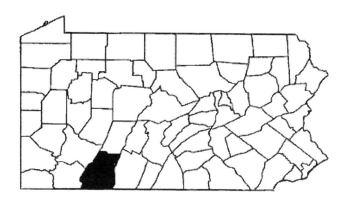

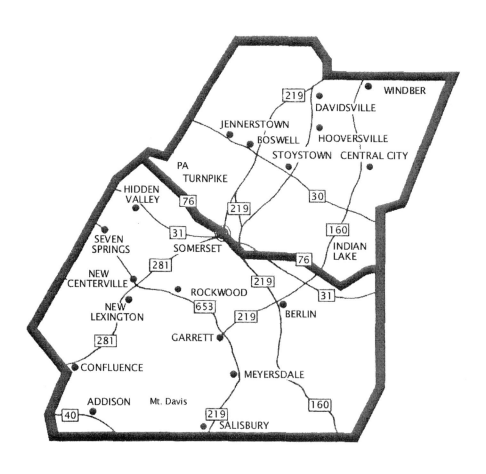

Somerset County

FOREWORD

Consider some of the gems of nature: a skein of geese flying above the golden and orange hues of autumn leaves, fields of wildflowers and their attendant butterflies, bees busily gathering pollen, a water snake gliding down a stream, the night hoot of an owl. How about lightning bugs (or lightning!), darting brook trout, salamanders under bark slabs, dewy spiderwebs, or a dawn chorus of birds . . . the wonders of nature seemingly have no end. Surprising as it is, some people take little notice of such things. Still others seem to appreciate them only after traveling to a distant place far from home. As enjoyable as touring certainly can be, residents of Somerset County, Pennsylvania, are really separated from a perpetually fascinating wild creation by only the walls around them. Just step outside, and see the world.

There is an interesting aspect to the allure of those wild things mentioned above. A person need know nothing of the identity or biology of the creatures involved to find themselves enchanted by them in the same manner as is the experienced naturalist. But after an initial introduction, many of us discover ourselves curious to learn more about those creatures or plants that intrigue us. "What are they? How do I distinguish them? Where do they live?" Hence the advent and popularity of guidebooks such as the *Peterson Field Guides* and the *Audubon Society Field Guides*. Roger Tory Peterson published *A Field Guide to the Birds* in 1934, and that book – the first modern field guide – inspired a series of guides that today cover more than fifty subjects from amphibians to wildflowers and sell millions the world over.

Most available guidebooks describe species found either throughout the United States or regionally, such as the eastern or northeastern United States. These helpful books provide most desired identifications for our region. But even a book dedicated to just "Pennsylvania" still leaves the reader imagining that the subjects treated are *elsewhere* and possibly far away from where they are sitting since many species are listed in those manuals that do not occur statewide. The purpose of this book, then, is to "bring it home": a focus on what is in **Somerset County** leaves no room for question. The flora and fauna discussed are here . . . here in our own backyards and not very far from the print of this page. As residents of Somerset County, we host, or are hosted by, a rich legacy of the natural world. This compilation will enable readers to become more aware of just what sort of plants and animals occur locally, and hopefully help us all to become more able stewards of their wonders.

How To Use This Guide:

I've tried to address two main questions: which species are actually in Somerset County *and* how common or uncommon they are. As many guidebooks already exist to aid in identifying our thousands of species, illustrations of them all are neither practical nor necessary. Likewise, biographies for the wild things living here are easily found in available books. So then, this book is best used in conjunction with field guides and natural history references for the many different forms of life that may be studied. If a person finds, say, a flower or salamander in the field and wants to know what it is, then using this reference will help to "rule in" or "rule out" the identification from the long lists of species covered in field guides. A sense of *what to look for* is thus gained, as well as how unusual the find might be.

The checklist format allows readers to better keep track of what they've seen. You should write in this book and make notations of dates and locations (or whatever you deem appropriate information) in the margins. That information will be useful for re-location, status assessment, or simply remembering a pleasant outing years down the road.

Field guides are useful for more than just in the field. Beginning students should select guide titles that interest them and try reading the guides as a break during the day, at lunch, or at bedtime. The more a person has read prior to exploring woods, fields, or wetlands, the better prepared they will be to make quick identifications once there.

Scientific keys, focusing on technical characters, have long been the gold standard for identifying organisms, but such keys are often tedious for those without formal training in using them. Visual approach guides are much more appealing to most people and the following sets are very popular aides in identifying much of our wildlife:

> **Peterson Field Guide Series:** usually the best for identification purposes
> **Audubon Society Field Guides:** beautiful photographs and more descriptive information
> **Golden Press Guides:** charming little introductory books and a few nice field guides as well

Use more than one reference if you can. Once enough experience is obtained in a given area, the scientific keys may start to become attractive as well. A respectable library of all these books can be

FOREWORD

assembled relatively cheaply through online auction sources such as eBay® and Amazon.com®. Also try Half.com® for low priced guides, or Bookfinder.com® for unusual titles. In addition, some of the best and most current guides to various subjects are not part of any series – see the **Sources** listed in each chapter for some of these. And don't forget to check the local public libraries that have nature books to lend.

Every chapter in this book also provides an introduction to the natural field covered within it by supplying the reader with information basic to the topic. Subdivisions within those chapters highlight knowledge that is especially useful or intriguing about the subjects. There is a little variation, but most chapters of flora and fauna are organized in a similar fashion:

General: introduces the class of biota and gives a sketch of biology and biography.

Facts & Figures: relates some interesting information for that topic; a few myths are dispelled as well.

Terms of Interest: defines selected terms that are frequently heard. Grit your teeth and learn the technical terms in the books you read – they will add considerably to your enjoyment of the topic.

Activities: suggestions on outdoor activities for individuals, couples, families, or kids.

County Status: codes are established for each species in context of its occurrence in Somerset County. Most codes are tailored individually for that section as differences exist for observation style and exploring technique for each type of plant or animal. Some chapters use more codes, some fewer.

Species: lists all the known species for the county by English and Latin names in conjunction with [sometimes subjective] **status codes** assigned to them. Most sections follow a *phylogenetic order* – a sequence based on genetic relativity – to at least the family level. Some chapters then list genera and species alphabetically in order to facilitate ease of location. The genus and species together comprise the Latin or *scientific* name. This name is considered incomplete without its author(s) listed immediately after it, but these authors were omitted in this text. They may be determined by referencing the sources listed.

Reviewed by: to ensure accuracy, each section was submitted to, and reviewed by an authority or authorities on the given subject. Mistakes, however, all belong to the author!

Sources: books, magazines, and other resources used in creation of the section are listed. Those references that are especially outstanding for local exploration are boldfaced.

Photos: a gallery in the back of the book showcases just a few of our many impressive species.

Most chapters are comprehensive up to publication (2002) in regards to species coverage. All could be added to, and each account of species begins with an estimate of the likelihood of that event **in the next few years** (with enough time, virtually all species are locally possible). Codes for each species were variously derived through personal experience, reviewers' experiences, local expertise, and general literature references. The benefit of having this information available is that users may formulate a list of that which is likely, and temporarily ignore those species that are not listed as occurring here. The pitfall, of course, would be in the event that a user encountered an unlisted species and then failed to consider it as a possibility in the process of establishing identification. As long as this limitation is understood, there is little problem. In fact, if someone should find any specimens that are not already listed as occurring in the county, then that person has a prize that this author and others might be keenly interested in hearing about.

Words of wisdom: to begin is the thing. Examine clouds or wildflowers *today*, listen to birdsong *today*, obtain a butterfly guide *today*, drop a hook in the water *today*. Once you're rolling, don't waste too much time on the specimens that you can't identify – there are plenty out there that are more easily mastered. Many of my own field finds were, not by choice, left to mystery in preparation of this book. Also remember the sage advice: "major on the majors, minor on the minors." Don't fret about separating warbler call notes, spore case arrangements of hybrid ferns, or caddisfly larvae until you've naturally ascended to that level of detail. Focus on bigger pictures when you begin and, moreover, you should simply *enjoy* your study thoroughly. The natural high that comes with finding a "life bird", a new snake, or your first gentian is a feeling that makes any given day memorable indeed.

I should add a cautionary note: it is only human nature to be drawn to things rare. We tend to want what we don't have, and especially what others don't have! Because of this, flora and fauna that are few in number often attract a lot of attention. Enthusiasts of any given class of biota may then become the unlikely perpetrators of the demise of rare populations. By repeatedly entering and altering sensitive habitats, we may literally "love them to death." Rare owls draw crowds that bother the birds, rare reptiles and amphibians are disturbed or collected for sale, rare nesting birds act as magnets to birders, and rare orchids get uprooted. So please be careful and exercise due diligence regarding your impact upon such species. And remember . . . the common species are often just as beautiful and worthy of attention as are the unusual ones – look for the beauty in everything. What's more, the species that flourish are the ones deserving respect for their ability to thrive in the unforgiving arena of natural selection.

To see, you must look. A small group of five friends and I were hiking through the woods several years ago as we headed for a rattlesnake den in Somerset County. We stopped to rest along the old road we'd been following, and then sat in a circle before going through the final piece of woods to search the den site. As sometimes happens, stories were traded and eventually one of us related how he and another fellow had once sat similarly elsewhere and had a **copperhead** perched right above their heads without even knowing it. That story just finished, we all laughed at the evident ignorance involved and there was a brief silence. Then all of a sudden "Hey, look at this . . ." A black phase **timber rattlesnake** sat coiled quietly among the leaf litter, square in the center of our circle. Here we were, a bunch of capable outdoorsmen going searching for snakes – veterans of thousands of such expeditions between us – and that rattlesnake had gone unnoticed at all our feet for a full five minutes. Since we were not yet at the place where we expected snakes, we had not yet begun to look, and therefore we had not seen. A trick to finding some of the pearls of the natural world is to not stop looking.

The Names:

Each species is listed with a Latin genus and species designation in *Italics* after it. This classification system is very basic to the study of living things and was instituted by a Swedish naturalist named Carl von Linné in 1753. The first name he Latinized was his own – he changed it to Linnaeus – and his *binomial nomenclature system* (two names for a given organism: genus and species) is often referred to as Linnaean classification. Incidentally, our culture uses a binomial system in naming people. Our last names identify us as a member of a clan; our first names specify a particular member of that clan.

Geographical differences in even just one county can produce many slang names for a given species of animal or plant. But the halls of science assign one genus/species Latin name that is constant the world over. Biologists in Russia, Germany, Brazil and America all recognize *Tyto alba* as one species – that we call in English **"Barn Owl"** and the French call "Effraie des Clochers" (and so on). The system works very well for the most part. Of course, people being imperfect makes it difficult to create any perfect system. In all the classes of all the phyla, there is such variability in many of the species that researchers sometimes disagree on the scientific naming and separation of them. In any event, the reader will likely learn a fair amount of the Latin language (plus many Greek roots) and gain insights about any given species if a little extra time is taken to learn the Latin names.

Identifying and naming organisms is **taxonomy.** Orderly arrangement of those groups to reflect their relatedness is **classification.** And **systematics** is the study of the diversity of living organisms and their evolutionary interrelationships through time.

In the following example, the **eastern garter snake** (*Thamnophis sirtalis sirtalis*) is used to demonstrate the basic hierarchy of groupings of organisms. Each subdivision is usually one of many subdivisions of the classification above it such that the end result is sort of a pyramid with the Kingdom on top branching downwards like an inverted family tree. It also could be likened to the armed forces with a bunch of privates under one sergeant, a bunch of sergeants under one major and so forth until we get to one general above them all.

Kingdom: Animalia	=	animals
Phylum: Chordata	=	animals with notochords
Class: Reptilia	=	reptiles
Order: Squamata	=	scaled reptiles
Family: Colubridae	=	colubrid snakes ("typical")
Genus: *Thamnophis*	=	Garter and Ribbon Snakes
Species: *sirtalis*	=	Common Garter Snake
Subspecies: *sirtalis*	=	Eastern subspecies of CGS

[A mnemonic: **K**ing **P**hillip **C**ame **O**ver **F**rom **G**reece **S**eeking **S**ilver]

FOREWORD

In order to further distinguish similar groups of biota from other groups, the prefixes *sub-* or *super-* are sometimes placed before any of the phyla through the families. For example, snakes are in the suborder *Serpentes* that separates them from other scaled reptiles such as lizards. While the subspecies designation is commonly employed with animals, two other divisions are used to further classify a given plant below the species level: *varieties* and *forms*. Note that genus names are capitalized and species designations usually are not.

What, then, is a species? A concrete definition is a bit difficult since nature will neither read nor obey it. Any definition will have exceptions and that is partly why taxonomy is always in a state of flux. But generally speaking, a **species** is a taxonomic group of related organisms or populations that are capable of breeding with each other and producing fertile offspring.

Some readers may notice that the text parts of most chapters present common names in all lower case letters. But the chapter covering the birds has first letters capitalized for common names of specific species. This reflects the conventional use of upper case letters in ornithology. The standard for all other natural disciplines is lower case. [Upper case letters were used for all species lists in each chapter as a simple stylistic preference.]

The following taxonomy shows the upper levels of how covered species are grouped and arranged.

PROTOCTISTA KINGDOM:
Phylum Myxomycota: slime molds
Phylum Chlorophyta: green algae
FUNGAL KINGDOM:
Phylum Ascomycota: sac fungi (and lichens)
Phylum Basidiomycota: club fungi
Phylum Zygomycota: bread molds
PLANT KINGDOM:
Phylum Bryophyta: mosses and liverworts
Phylum Pteridophyta: club mosses, horsetails, quillworts, ferns
Phylum Spermatophyta: seed-bearing plants
    Class Angiospermae (or Magnoliophyta): flowering plants
    Class Gymnospermae (or Pinophyta): conifers (cone-bearing plants)
ANIMAL KINGDOM:
Phylum Cnidaria: jellyfish
Phylum Ectoprocta: bryozoans (moss animals)
Phylum Mollusca: slugs, snails
Phylum Platyhelminthes: flatworms
Phylum Annelida: worms, leeches
Phylum Arthropoda: insects, arachnids, crustaceans, and myriapods (centipedes, et al.)
Phylum Chordata: animals with notochords *in at least one phase* of their life cycle (includes mammals, birds, fish, etc… Sub-phylum *Vertebrata* contains most of classes in this phylum; vertebrates have a *backbone*)

There are also other kingdoms and phyla present. Remember that this book doesn't cover the many thousands of microscopic organisms occurring locally. It should be noted that there are about 1.75 million described species worldwide. Somerset County's Verizon telephone book has close to 79,000 entries in the local white pages. So it would take more than 21 of those sections just to list all of the species known to science! Additionally, best guesses by scientists put the estimate *at least* around *13-14 million* species that exist (~eight times the known). The world about us is literally pulsing with life.

For those interested, the following two websites are both excellent places to learn more about taxonomy, classification, and systematics:
World Biodiversity Database wwweti.eti.bio.uva.nl/Database/WBD.html
Tree of Life phylogeny.arizona.edu/tree/life.html

Many creatures and plants live their lives within our borders and have thus far remained undetected. It is likely that more species will be discovered and added on even while this book is being printed. Make your own space for them if found and, if possible, submit details to interested authorities.

FOREWORD

Dedication:

Many thanks and much love goes to my wife, Jill, and our boys for their help. I owe a special debt of gratitude to Jill for assistance, general counsel, encouragement, and for sharing in nature with me. Thanks to my children, Nicholas, Andrew, and James for helping me to remember the miracle of life and the magic of nature (like the allure of frogs). Thanks to them, too, for accompanying me on collections and picture-taking rounds, catching specimens, and critiquing many photos. Thanks to my parents, W. Robert and Susan Bastian, for introducing me to the outdoors and supporting my interests. Most importantly, thanks to Jesus Christ . . . for to me He ultimately gives it all meaning.

Acknowledgements:

I am deeply indebted to **all of the reviewers** listed here and in each chapter – their advice, opinions, and abilities were invaluable. They are: Kevin B. Baker, Richard A. Bradley, Ph.D., Doris L. Brown, Ph.D., Robert A. Byers, Ph.D., Richard C. Ely, James A. Hart, Arthur C. Hulse, Ph.D., Daniel W. Jenkins, Steven G. Johnson, Carl S. Keener, Ph.D., Robert C. Leberman, Dennis L. Mammana, Anthony J. Marich, Jr., Joseph F. Merritt, Ph.D., Robert S. Mulvihill, M.S., James C. Parks, Ph.D., John R. Plischke III, John E. Rawlins, Ph.D., Gary A. Smith, Scott W. Tomlinson, and Brian D. Wolff.

Special thanks are due to Dr. Carl Keener and Robert Leberman for generously editing large portions of the manuscript. Dr. Keener also assisted in identifying specimens. John Plischke III shared his numerous county fungal records. Richard Bradley, Ph.D. furnished arachnid identifications. Steve Johnson supplied scores of county Lepidoptera records and much assistance with specimens. Gary Smith provided most records and codes for fishes. Thomas "Nick" Donnelly, Ph.D. supplied his Odonata records.

Additional Support:

I'm much obliged to: my in-laws Lowell and Carna Friedline (and family) for preserving their marvelous wetlands and sharing many interesting finds, Jason Collins for general assistance, and the Somerset Wal-Mart Photo crew for their fine service. Also, the following people provided information, status review, or records, which helped to make each chapter a little (or a lot) better:

Mushrooms: Thomas Chulick, Ken Lohr, Scott A. Redhead, Ph.D.
Grasses, Sedges, & Rushes: Brian Wolff (Wildlife Habitat Biologist, NRCS)
Wildflowers: Ralph Barnett, W. Robert Bastian D.V.M., Robert Leberman, Anthony Marich, Jr., Ralph Mostoller, Bob Mulvihill, M.S., Peggy Wisner
Trees & Shrubs: Lynette Ely, Larry Powell (Appalachian Forest Consultants)
Arachnids: Steve Jacobs, M.S. (Penn State University Extension)
Insects: Bob Brown, Miquel Saviroff (County Agricultural Extension), John Seth (Ehrlich Pest Control)
Butterflies & Moths: Sally Dick, M.D., Bob Mulvihill, M.S.
Fishes: Larry Jackson & Tim Wilson (PA Fish & Boat Commission Biologists), Lewis "Skip" Shafer, O.D.
Amphibians: Jeff Payne, D.V.M., Leroy "Whitey" Shaller
Reptiles: Ken Stairs (many trips to the woods over the years), Doug Walters
Birds: Jillynn Bastian, Tom Dick, D.V.M., Anthony Marich, Jr., Richard Murphy, Jeff Payne, D.V.M. (lots of records and codes), Lauretta Payne, D.V.M., Ruth Sager
Mammals: Jim Griffith, Andrew Lutz (PA Turnpike), Chris Sanders, W.C.O. John Smith
Additional Species: Ted Nuttall, Ph.D., Tim Vechter, John Wolff
Foreword: Dennis O'Neil, Ph.D. (taxonomy)

Sherren Pensiero, The Write Solution, deserves my thanks for her editing skills and assistance.

Lastly, there are many un-named people who were important in the production of this book in one way or another. I have not forgotten them and I'd like to thank them all.

Nature study acts as a soothing balm; "it is a marvelous tonic to the pace and pressures of this early twenty-first century. ***Your antidote awaits you.****" Read, explore, learn, and enjoy!*

"And God saw everything that He had made,
and,
behold,
it was very good."

Genesis 1:31a
(King James Version)

Types of Habitat in Somerset County:

These are the most common habitat types found in our county. Small patches of other habitat types exist, as well as subdivisions among those listed. To learn more about habitats and ecology, try the easy-reading book entitled *The Field Guide to Wildlife Habitats of the Eastern United States* by Janine M. Benyus. Each habitat has its own distinct communities and associations of plants and creatures within.

LAKE AND POND

Common habitat – there are countless small ponds around the county.

CATTAIL MARSH

Check the edges of the big lakes for these. Lake Somerset has an abundance of **cattail** vegetation. **Cattails** are sometimes thought of as a nuisance wetland species as they choke out competitors.

SHRUB SWAMP

Sometimes difficult to negotiate (dense vegetation), but productive for a great variety of biota.

BOG AND BOG FOREST

Rare locally, but there are small bogs around Mt. Davis and on Laurel Mountain. Certain plants and animals thrive only under these acidic soil conditions.

NORTHERN FLOODPLAIN FOREST

Small areas of this habitat type are found along the shores of flood-prone rivers.

GRASSY FIELD

Good examples of this habitat are reclaimed strip mine area, which abound in the county. Many grassland birds are attracted to these prairie-like environs.

ABANDONED FIELD

Desirable habitat for many species: with the decline in small farms, numerous agricultural fields are reverting to old-field style habitat that progresses over time to woodlands.

SHRUB-SAPLING OPENING EDGE

Wherever there are woods there are also wooded edges and these areas are especially appealing to many birds, insects, mammals, and more.

TRANSITION FOREST

Pockets of this habitat are scattered around the county (mostly **sugar maple** and **hemlock** mix).

OAK-HICKORY FOREST

Abundant: the most common woodland type we have.

LIMESTONE OUTCROPPINGS

Uncommon: these areas often yield unusual flora for the county.

NEEDLELEAF STANDS & PLANTATIONS

Nice stands of **hemlock** and **pine** are found in addition to many large stands of planted conifers. These wooded areas are very appealing to owls and various other birds, mushrooms, moths, etc.

MIXED DECIDUOUS

Conifers mixed in with broadleaf trees. Certain species are partial to this habitat type.

TOWNS

This is preferred habitat for various species. **Chimney Swifts** and **Nighthawks** are most easily found in towns – Somerset is good for both. Night-flying moths are often attracted to pole lights in towns and smaller mammals may find safe harbor in towns where some predators cannot reside or hunt.

Reviewed by:

Richard C. Ely – Registered Professional Geologist
Anthony J. Marich, Jr. – Surface Mine Conservation Inspector, District 56
Brian D. Wolff – Wildlife Habitat Biologist, Natural Resources Conservation Service

Sources:

Benyus, Janine M. 1989. *The Field Guide to Wildlife Habitats of the Eastern United States*. Simon &
   Schuster, New York. 336 pp.
USDA. 1983. *Soil Survey of Somerset County Pennsylvania*. United States Department of Agriculture &
   Soil Conservation Service. 148 pp.

Map:

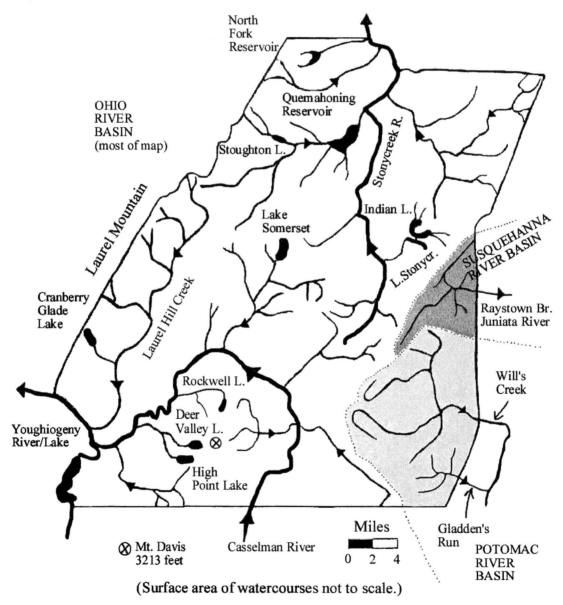

(Surface area of watercourses not to scale.)

Figure 1 – Basic Somerset County Hydrography

MUSHROOMS & FUNGI of Somerset County, PA

General:

Once considered to be in the plant kingdom, fungi are now classified in a separate kingdom due to their unique biology. Although there are at least 75,000 species worldwide, undoubtedly there are many more than that. Unlike green plants that produce their own sustenance, fungi derive their food from the decay of wood, soil, manure, animal protein or leaf litter (parasitic) – or even living plant and animal tissues (saprophytic). Fungi are vital in their role as decomposers.

Similar to ferns, fungi reproduce with spores rather than seeds. Billions of microscopic spores fall from a typical mushroom, which can then develop into structures called *hyphae*. These, in turn, form a *mycelium* (vegetative state) from which the *mushroom* (the "fruiting body") develops. Fungi have many shapes, with the classic toadstools as one common example. The focus here is on our macroscopic, or easily seen, fungi, and omits nearly the entire multitude of microscopic organisms, e.g., the **ringworm** fungi of animals, the **American chestnut blight fungus,** and *Saccharomyces cerevisiae* – the yeast of the baking and brewing industries. Molds, mildews, rusts, and smuts are also members of the fungal kingdom, but they may require microscopic or chemical separations to establish species identification.

Many of the common names used to describe the mushrooms are quite descriptive, and some are rather ominous **(witches' butter, destroying angel, dead man's fingers).** But the rainbow of colors and plethora of interesting forms dispel any notion of foreboding when the fungi are studied. From the delicate charm of the **pinwheel marasmius** or **bird's nest fungus** (a more fitting name is hard to imagine) to the fiery orange of a **Caesar's mushroom** or **chicken-of-the-woods,** there is a broad array of fascinating fungi in our county. Many local outdoorsmen are familiar with a few of the classic edibles: with a little effort, plenty of the more common mushrooms become known by name.

Identification of mushrooms is often challenging. Some determinations require a careful study of the microscopic reproductive spores. And certain types vex even the experts. But many of our mushrooms are easily identifiable on sight by their physical characteristics; so don't be intimidated by the tough ones – everything that is found need not be identified. Size, shape, structure, color, smell, taste (experts only), habitat, and spore print are all useful in identification. Spore prints are produced by placing a mushroom cap on either white or black paper for several hours. Spore color is necessary when determining difficult species and the practice of making a print should become habit whenever a questionable species is found.

Fungi demonstrate how important it can be to utilize more than one book. There is considerable variation in nomenclature from one text to another, plus many varieties are covered in one guide but not in others. So refer to multiple books and compare the scientific names, which are more apt to resemble one another. The *Audubon Guide* (Lincoff) is perhaps the most widely used. Harder to find and more expensive – but really the best available for our region – is the guide *Mushrooms of Northeastern North America* (Bessette et al.). *Mushrooms Demystified* (Arora) is an entertaining and valuable reference.

Where & When:

Start looking for fungi in your back yard. Pastures and orchards can be productive – check woodlands in particular. Certain types are found year around, but autumn produces the largest variety. Wet weather is especially good for mushrooms and an autumn rainstorm after a dry spell is certain to yield bountiful results. Stumps, parks, lawns, manure, dead trees, and forest floors all have something to offer. Many mushrooms prefer certain kinds of wood as substrate. So check out different woodlands for different species. Timing can be critical as fruiting may last only a few days. Keep all your senses alert: once you learn the smell of stinkhorns, you may well determine their presence in an area long before you spot them.

There are folks, "pothunters," who enjoy eating many of the mushrooms to be found in the wild and, indeed, some are very tasty when prepared properly. Foremost among the hunted around our area are the **morels, hen-of-the-woods,** and **meadow mushroom** – locally referred to as **"spongies, sheep's head, and pinkies"** respectively. The season for edibles begins in mid-April **(black morels),** continues in August **(pinkies),** and winds down in October **(sheep's head).** Ask a morel hunter where they find their mushrooms and you'll most likely be told "in the woods" as productive sites are jealously guarded. Apple orchards, burned areas, and ash trees are favored spots for morels. Mushrooms often grow true to an area as the mycelium (comparable to both the root and plant of a flower) may last for many years underground.

A nickel's worth of free advice . . . eating wild mushrooms is a game for experts and caution should be the watchword as even the delicious **common morel** has potentially poisonous look-alikes **(false morels)** found in the county. Heed the sage advice: "There are *old* mushroom hunters and there are *bold* mushroom hunters. But there are *no old, bold* mushroom hunters!"

MUSHROOMS & FUNGI of Somerset County, PA

Facts & Figures;

➤ Mushrooms grow fast. They may appear literally overnight.

➤ The manure-loving **gray shag** liquefies to black ink within 15 minutes of being picked!

➤ The **common tumbling puffballs** ("smoke-bombs" to kids) that are found all over the area are legendary for inducing blindness. This isn't so, but their powder would certainly irritate the eyes.

➤ **Fairy ring mushrooms** were long ago thought to be the result of evening dances by "little people."

➤ **Chanterelles** are probably the most prized and popular edible mushrooms worldwide.

➤ A **giant puffball** contains up to 7,000,000,000,000 (that's seven *trillion*!) spores.

➤ The ancients suspected Zeus's lightning to be the cause of mushroom growth, as they could neither find seeds nor grow them in cultivation; but they were able to find them after a good thunderstorm (moisture).

➤ Psilocybe mushrooms are hallucinogenic; they include the "shrooms" that buzz-seekers abuse.

➤ **Amanitas** (e.g., **destroying angel**) are involved in 90% of fatal mushroom poisonings – one bite can be fatal. That event has happened on more than one occasion in Somerset County.

➤ Commercial mushrooms found in the store and on your pizza (*Agaricus bisporus*) are grown in caves.

➤ Sir Alexander Fleming discovered the antibiotic penicillin. It was originally isolated from a mold fungus called *Penicillium* that was growing on a sliced orange.

Additional Folklore:

False notions abound regarding mushrooms – most pertain to edibility. One such notion is that if a silver spoon is put into a pot of boiling water with a mushroom and then turns black, the mushroom is poisonous. Some use the presence of a "poison cup" at the base of the stalk or a ring on the stem to diagnose edibility or the lack thereof. Others claim that edible mushroom caps peel easily. These ideas should all be regarded as **useless** in spite of some valid reasons for their origins. The term "toadstool" is colloquial for poisonous varieties of mushroom, but is often applied to any mushroom by more than a few.

Some Terms of Interest:

Mycology	the study of fungi; a *mycologist* is a scientist who studies fungi
Mycelium	the vegetative portion of a fungus – grows underground
Bolete	fleshy mushrooms with porous, tube-like layers on undersurface of cap
Bruising	when the gills of certain species are traumatized, they may dramatically turn color
Cap	head or top part of a mushroom (*stalk* is the stem)
Cup/Volva	"poison cup" – sac tissue at stalk base of some mushrooms (e.g., **Amanitas**)
"LBM"	Little Brown Mushroom – generic term for many species that are so described
Gills	radial series of spore-bearing blades on the undersurface of mushroom caps
Ring	remnant of veil after separation – located on upper stalk; also called *annulus*
Mycorrhiza	symbiotic association of fungus and plant roots (important to orchids and many others)
Veil	tissue that protects immature parts of some mushrooms and boletes
Spore Print	color and pattern made by spores dropped by cap on paper – used in identification

Activities:

• On the chapter list, check all of the fungi that you have found. Make notes on where and when.

• Draw a picture on nature's etch-a-sketch . . . the **artist's conk.**

• Order **morels** or **truffles** (a European origin mushroom) at a nice restaurant or specialty foods shop.

• Leave the cap of a picked mushroom sit on paper awhile and check for the color print formed by spores.

• Check old mushrooms for smaller mushrooms that may grow upon them.

• **Jack o'lantern** earns its name by more than the pumpkin-orange color; take a freshly picked one into a dark room and see the gills glow green.

• You can test for **"milkies"** by running a sharp twig through the gills of typical shaped mushrooms in the fall and watch to see if beads of a milky latex solution exude from the wounds created. In similar fashion; press on the spongy underpart of a found bolete to see if it is one of the species that bruises blue.

• Contact the North American Mycological Association at 4245 Redinger Road, Portsmouth, Ohio 45662 or at www.namyco.org for more information about fungi and the study of them.

• Join the Western Pennsylvania Mushroom Club; visit at www.wpmc4.homestead.com/index.html.

County Status Codes:

Common   routinely encountered – these are usually found easily in appropriate habitat and season
Fairly Common familiar mushrooms; should be found by the persistent seeker
Uncommon   sporadically found; typically requires an effort over time to locate
Occasional   often difficult to find; a lot of searching . . . or you may get lucky!
Rare   one or few records for the county

Names, common and scientific, were mostly taken from *Mushrooms of Northeastern North America* (Bessette, et al.) and/or the *Audubon Society Guide* (Lincoff). Taxonomic hierarchy employed is a "patchwork" and reflects the current state of uncertainty in this area. Former or alternate taxonomic names are noted in some cases in parentheses. Check the website www.ukncc.co.uk/cabipages/Names/fundic.asp for information in determining current fungal classifications. Families and genera appear alphabetically.

Species: [262] Additions are likely – many more harder-to-find species certainly occur.

Phylum Ascomycota – Sac Fungi
Class Discomycetes – Disc Fungi

Order Pezizales – Cup Fungi & allies [24]

		Status
Orange Peel	*Aleuria aurantia*	fairly common
Burn Cups	*Anthracobia maurilabia*	occasional
Hairy Rubber Cup	*Galiella rufa*	occasional
Saddle-shaped False Morel	*Gyromitra infula*	uncommon
Korf's Morel	*Gyromitra korfii*	uncommon
Fluted White Helvella	*Helvella crispa*	fairly common
Long Stalked Gray Cup	*Helvella macropus*	fairly common
Shaggy Scarlet Cup	*Microstoma floccosa*	uncommon
Pecks Morel	*Morchella angusticeps*	uncommon
Thick Footed Morel	*Morchella crassipes*	uncommon
White Morel	*Morchella deliciosa*	uncommon
Black Morel	*Morchella elata*	uncommon
Common (or Yellow) Morel	*Morchella esculenta*	uncommon
Half Free Morel	*Morchella semilibera*	uncommon
Bladder Cup	*Peziza vesciculosa*	occasional
Tar Spot of Maple	*Rhytisma acerinum*	occasional
Scarlet Cup	*Sarcoscypha austriaca*	occasional
Stalked Scarlet Cup	*Sarcoscypha occidentalis*	fairly common
Burn Eyelash Cup	*Scutellinia brunnea*	uncommon
Eyelash Cup	*Scutellinia scutellata*	fairly common
Elf Cup	*Tarzetta cupularis*	uncommon
Devil's Urn	*Urnula craterium*	fairly common
Smooth Thimble Cap	*Verpa conica*	uncommon
Moose's Antlers	*Wynnea americana*	rare

Order Helotiales – Earth Tongues [10]

Purple Jelly Drops	*Ascocoryne sarcoides*	uncommon
Yellow Fairy Cups	*Bisporella citrina*	fairly common
Black Jelly Drops	*Bulgaria inquinans*	occasional
Green Stain	*Chlorociboria aeruginascens*	occasional
Stalked Hairy Fairy Cup	*Dasyscyphus virgineus*	common
Ochre Jelly Club	*Leotia lubrica*	occasional
Green Headed Jelly Club	*Leotia viscosa*	uncommon
Swamp Beacon	*Mitrula elegans (paludosa)*	occasional
Irregular Earth Tongue	*Neolecta irregularis*	uncommon
Water Club	*Vibrissea truncorum*	uncommon

Class Pyrenomycetes

Order Sphaeriales – Ostiole Flasks [13]   Status

____	Headlike Cordyceps	*Cordyceps capitata*	uncommon
____	Beetle Cordyceps	*Cordyceps melolonthae*	uncommon
____	Trooping Cordyceps	*Cordyceps militaris*	uncommon
____	Goldenthread Cordyceps	*Cordyceps ophioglossoides*	uncommon
____	Carbon Balls	*Daldinia concentrica*	common
____	Yellow Cushion Hypocrea	*Hypocrea (Creopus) gelatinosa*	common
____	Golden Hypomyces	*Hypomyces chrysospermus*	common
____	Amanita Mold	*Hypomyces hyalinus*	common
____	Yellow Green Hypomyces	*Hypomyces luteovirens*	occasional
____	Red Cushion Hypoxylon	*Hypoxylon fragiforme*	occasional
____	Carbon Cushion	*Ustulina deusta*	occasional
____	Carbon Antlers	*Xylaria hypoxylon*	uncommon
____	Dead Man's Fingers	*Xylaria polymorpha*	common

Phylum Basidiomycota – Club Fungi

Class Ustomycetes

Order Ustilaginales – Smuts [1]

____	Corn Smut	*Ustilago maydis*	common

Class Teliomycetes

Order Uredinales – Rusts [4]

____	Goldenrod Rust	*Coleosporium asterum*	uncommon
____	Orange Rust	*Gymnoconia peckiana*	common
____	Spring Beauty Rust	*Puccinia mariae-wilsoni*	rare
____	Jack-in-the-Pulpit Rust	*Uromyces ari-triphylli*	rare

Class Hymenomycetes – Exposed Hymenium Fungi

Order Tremellales – Jelly Fungi [6]

____	Tree-Ear	*Auricularia auricula*	occasional
____	Orange Jelly	*Dacrymyces palmatus*	uncommon
____	Black Jelly Roll	*Exidia glandulosa*	uncommon
____	Leaf Jelly	*Tremella foliacea*	occasional
____	Witches' Butter	*Tremella mesenterica (lutescens)*	uncommon
____	False Coral	*Tremellodendron pallidum (schweinitzii)*	fairly common

Order Aphyllophorales – Coral & Pore Fungi & allies

CHANTERELLE FAMILY – Cantherellaceae [7]

____	Chanterelle	*Cantharellus cibarius*	uncommon
____	Cinnabar-red Chanterelle	*Cantharellus cinnabarinus*	uncommon
____	Smooth Chanterelle	*Cantharellus lateritius*	uncommon
____	Small Chanterelle	*Cantharellus minor*	occasional
____	Trumpet Chanterelle	*Cantharellus tubaeformis*	uncommon
____	Black Trumpet	*Craterellus fallax*	uncommon
____	Scaly Vase Chanterelle	*Gomphus floccosus*	uncommon

CORAL FUNGUS FAMILY – Clavariaceae [11]

____	White Worm Coral	*Clavaria vermicularis*	occasional
____	Flat-topped Coral	*Clavariadelphus truncatus*	uncommon
____	Crown-tipped Coral	*Clavicorona pyxidata*	fairly common

CORAL FUNGUS FAMILY – continued

	Common Name	Scientific Name	Status
____	Violet-branched Coral	*Clavulina amethystina*	occasional
____	Gray Coral	*Clavulina cinerea*	fairly common
____	Crested Coral	*Clavulina cristata*	occasional
____	Spindle-shaped Yellow Coral	*Clavulinopsis fusiformis*	fairly common
____	White Green-algae Coral	*Multiclavula mucida*	occasional
____	Straight-branched Coral	*Ramaria stricta*	common
____	Eastern Cauliflower Mushroom	*Sparassis herbstii (crispa)*	occasional
____	Common Fiber Vase	*Thelephora terrestris*	occasional

DRY ROT FAMILY – Coniophoraceae [2]

____	Wet Rot	*Coniophora puteana*	fairly common
____	Dry Rot	*Serpula lacrimans*	fairly common

TOOTH FUNGUS FAMILY – Hydnaceae [9]

____	Pinecone Tooth	*Auriscalpium vulgare*	uncommon
____	Northern Tooth	*Climacodon septentrionale*	occasional
____	Sweet Tooth	*Dentinum (Hydnum) repandum*	occasional
____	Belly Button Tooth	*Dentinum (Hydnum) umbilicatum*	occasional
____	Bear's Head Tooth	*Hericium coralloides*	uncommon
____	Bearded Tooth	*Hericium erinaceus*	uncommon
____	Comb Tooth	*Hericium ramosum*	uncommon
____	Scaly Tooth	*Hydnum (Sarcodon) imbricatum*	uncommon
____	Ochre Spreading Tooth	*Steccherinum ochraceum*	fairly common

POLYPORE FAMILY – Polyporaceae [34]

____	Berkeley's Polypore	*Bondarzewia berkeleyi*	common
____	Mossy Maze Polypore	*Cerrena unicolor*	fairly common
____	Shiny Cinnamon Polypore	*Coltricia cinnamomea*	uncommon
____	Thick-maze Oak Polypore	*Daedalea quercina*	common
____	Thin-maze Flat Polypore	*Daedaleopsis confragosa*	common
____	Beefsteak Polypore	*Fistulina hepatica*	uncommon
____	Tinder Polypore	*Fomes fomentarius*	fairly common
____	Red-belted Polypore	*Fomitopsis pinicola*	fairly common
____	Artist's Conk	*Ganoderma applanatum*	common
____	Ling Chih	*Ganoderma lucidum*	fairly common
____	Hemlock Varnish Shelf	*Ganoderma tsugae*	common
____	Hen-of-the-Woods / "Sheep's Head"	*Grifola frondosa*	fairly common
____	Warted Oak Polypore	*Inonotus dryadeus*	occasional
____	Milk-white Toothed Polypore	*Irpex lacteus*	fairly common
____	Resinous Polypore	*Ischnoderma resinosum*	occasional
____	White Pored Chicken Mushroom	*Laetiporus cincinnatia*	uncommon
____	Chicken Mushroom	*Laetiporus sulphureus*	fairly common
____	Multicolor Gill Polypore	*Lenzites betulina*	fairly common
____	Black-staining Polypore	*Meripilus sumstinei (giganteus)*	uncommon
____	Dye Polypore	*Phaeolus schweinitzii*	uncommon
____	Flecked-flesh Polypore	*Phellinus igniarius*	uncommon
____	Cracked-cap Polypore	*Phellinus rimosus*	common
____	Birch Polypore	*Piptoporus betulinus*	common
____	Spring Polypore	*Polyporus arcularius*	common
____	Black-footed Polypore	*Polyporus badius*	common
____	Winter Polypore	*Polyporus brumalis*	occasional
____	Rooting Polypore	*Polyporus radicatus*	uncommon
____	Dryad's Saddle	*Polyporus squamosus*	common
____	Little Nest Polypore	*Poronidulus (Trametes) conchifer*	occasional

MUSHROOMS & FUNGI of Somerset County, PA

			Status
POLYPORE FAMILY – continued			
____	Cinnabar-red Polypore	*Pycnoporus cinnabarinus*	common
____	Turkeytail	*Trametes versicolor*	common
____	Violet-toothed Polypore	*Trichaptum biformis*	uncommon
____	Blue Cheese Polypore	*Tyromyces caesius*	uncommon
____	White Cheese Polypore	*Tyromyces chioneus*	occasional

SPLITGILL FAMILY – Schizophyllaceae [1]

____	Common Split Gill	*Schizophyllum commune*	fairly common

PARCHMENT FUNGUS FAMILY – Stereaceae [4]

____	Crowded Parchment	*Stereum complicatum*	common
____	False Turkeytail	*Stereum ostrea*	fairly common
____	Silky Parchment	*Stereum striatum*	fairly common
____	Ceramic Parchment	*Xylobolus frustulatus*	common

Order Agaricales – Agarics & Boletes

AGARICUS & LEPIOTA FAMILY – Agaricaceae [10]

____	Abruptly-bulbous Agaricus	*Agaricus abruptibulbus*	fairly common
____	Horse Mushroom	*Agaricus arvensis*	fairly common
____	Sidewalk Mushroom	*Agaricus bitorquis*	uncommon
____	Meadow Mushroom / "Pinkies"	*Agaricus campestris*	common
____	Eastern Prince	*Agaricus placomyces*	uncommon
____	Reddening Lepiota	*Lepiota americana*	fairly common
____	Onion-stalked Lepiota	*Lepiota cepaestipes*	occasional
____	Smooth Lepiota	*Lepiota naucina (naucinoides)*	fairly common
____	Parasol	*Lepiota (Macrolepiota) procera*	fairly common
____	Shaggy Parasol	*Lepiota (Macrolepiota) rachodes*	occasional

AMANITA FAMILY – Amanitaceae [10]

____	Cleft-foot Amanita	*Amanita brunnescens*	fairly common
____	Caesar's Mushroom	*Amanita caesarea*	fairly common
____	Citron Amanita	*Amanita citrina*	fairly common
____	Yellow Patches	*Amanita flavoconia*	fairly common
____	Tawny Grisette	*Amanita fulva*	occasional
____	Gemmed Amanita	*Amanita gemmata*	fairly common
____	Fly Agaric	*Amanita muscaria* var. *formosa*	fairly common
____	Blusher	*Amanita rubescens*	common
____	Grisette	*Amanita vaginata*	fairly common
____	Destroying Angel	*Amanita virosa*	fairly common

BOLBITIUS FAMILY – Bolbitiaceae [5]

____	Cracked Earthscale / Hard Agrocybe	*Agrocybe dura*	fairly common
____	Hemispheric Agrocybe	*Agrocybe pediades*	common
____	Yellow Bolbitius	*Bolbitius vitellinus*	occasional
____	Deadly Conocybe	*Conocybe filaris*	fairly common
____	White Dunce Cap	*Conocybe lactea*	uncommon

BOLETE FAMILY – Boletaceae [22]

____	Two-colored Bolete	*Boletus bicolor*	fairly common
____	Summer Redcap	*Boletus fraternus*	common
____	Frost's Bolete	*Boletus frostii*	fairly common
____	Noble Bolete	*Boletus nobilis*	fairly common
____	Goldstalk	*Boletus ornatipes*	fairly common

BOLETE FAMILY – continued

			Status
____	**Parasite Bolete**	*Boletus parasiticus*	uncommon
____	**King-like Bolete**	*Boletus subcaerulescens*	fairly common
____	**Red Mouth Bolete**	*Boletus subvelutipes*	fairly common
____	**Yellow-cracked Bolete**	*Boletus subtomentosus*	fairly common
____	**Ash-tree Bolete**	*Boletinellus (Gyrodon) merulioides*	common
____	**Chestnut Bolete**	*Gyroporus castaneus*	occasional
____	**Old-Man-of-the-Woods**	*Strobilomyces floccopus*	common
____	**Chicken-fat Suillus**	*Suillus americanus*	common
____	**Short-stalked Suillus**	*Suillus brevipes*	occasional
____	**Dotted-stalked Suillus**	*Suillus granulatus*	fairly common
____	**Larch Suillus**	*Suillus grevillei*	uncommon
____	**Slippery Jack**	*Suillus luteus*	common
____	**Painted Slipperycap**	*Suillus pictus*	fairly common
____	**Black Velvet Bolete**	*Tylopilus alboater*	uncommon
____	**Bitter Bolete**	*Tylopilus felleus*	common
____	**Violet-gray Bolete**	*Tylopilus plumbeoviolaceus*	fairly common
____	**Pink Bolete**	*Xanthoconium separans*	occasional

INKY CAP FAMILY – Coprinaceae [11]

____	**Alcohol Inky**	*Coprinus atramentarius*	occasional
____	**Gray Shag**	*Coprinus cinereus*	common
____	**Shaggy Mane**	*Coprinus comatus*	common
____	**Non-inky Coprinus**	*Coprinus disseminatus*	uncommon
____	**Mica Cap**	*Coprinus micaceus*	fairly common
____	**Japanese Umbrella Inky**	*Coprinus plicatilis*	fairly common
____	**Orange-mat Coprinus**	*Coprinus radians*	uncommon
____	**Girdled Panaeolus**	*Panaeolus subbalteatus*	fairly common
____	**Common Psathyrella**	*Psathyrella candolleana*	fairly common
____	**Lawn Mower's Mushroom**	*Psathyrella foenisecii*	fairly common
____	**Corrugated-cap Psathyrella**	*Psathyrella rugocephala*	occasional

CORTINARIUS FAMILY – Cortinariaceae [8]

____	**Bracelet Cort**	*Cortinarius armillatus*	fairly common
____	**Cinnabar Cort**	*Cortinarius cinnabarinus*	fairly common
____	**Heliotrope Cort**	*Cortinarius heliotropicus*	uncommon
____	**Viscid Violet Cort**	*Cortinarius iodes*	fairly common
____	**Red Gilled Cort**	*Cortinarius semisanguineus*	uncommon
____	**Deadly Galerina**	*Galerina autumnalis*	common
____	**Big Laughing Gym**	*Gymnopilus spectabilis*	uncommon
____	**Poison Pie**	*Hebeloma crustuliniforme*	uncommon

CREPIDOTUS FAMILY – Crepidotaceae [1]

____	**Flat Crep**	*Crepidotus applanatus*	fairly common

ENTOLOMA FAMILY – Entolomataceae [4]

____	**Aborted Entoloma**	*Entoloma abortivum*	uncommon
____	**Yellow Unicorn Entoloma**	*Nolanea murraii*	fairly common
____	**Salmon Unicorn Entoloma**	*Nolanea salmoneum (quadrata)*	fairly common
____	**Early Spring Entoloma**	*Nolanea verna*	fairly common

MUSHROOMS & FUNGI of Somerset County, PA

HYGROPHORUS FAMILY – Hygrophoraceae [5]   **Status**

____	Chanterelle Waxy Cap	*Hygrocybe (Hygophorus) cantherellus*	uncommon
____	Witch's Hat	*Hygrocybe (Hygophorus) conicus*	occasional
____	Golden Waxy Cap	*Hygrocybe (Hygophorus) flavescens*	uncommon
____	Orange-gilled Waxy Cap	*Hygrocybe (Hygrophorus) marginatus* var. *concolor*	uncommon
____	Fading Scarlet Waxy Cap	*Hygrocybe (Hygophorus) miniatus*	fairly common

PLUTEUS FAMILY – Pluteaceae [3]

____	Black-edged Pluteus	*Pluteus atromarginatus*	uncommon
____	Fawn Mushroom	*Pluteus cervinus*	common
____	Smooth Volvariella	*Volvariella speciosa*	occasional

RUSSULA FAMILY – Russulaceae [11]

____	Deceptive Milky	*Lactarius deceptivus*	common
____	Gerard's Milky	*Lactarius gerardii*	occasional
____	Peck's Milky	*Lactarius peckii*	fairly common
____	Variegated Milky	*Lactarius subpurpureus*	uncommon
____	Yellow-latex Milky	*Lactarius vinaceorufescens*	common
____	Tawny Milky	*Lactarius volemus*	uncommon
____	Tacky Green Russula	*Russula aeruginea*	common
____	Green Quilt Russula	*Russula crustosa*	fairly common
____	Purple-bloom Russula	*Russula mariae*	uncommon
____	Blackish-red Russula	*Russula krombholzii(atropurpurea)*	uncommon
____	Woodland Red Russula	*Russula silvicola*	common

STROPHARIA FAMILY – Strophariaceae [8]

____	Sulfur Tuft	*Hypholoma (Naematoloma) fasciculare*	occasional
____	Brick Tops	*Hypholoma(Naematoloma) sublateritium*	occasional
____	Powder-scale Pholiota	*Phaeomarasmius erinaceellus*	uncommon
____	Golden Pholiota / Goldskin Scalecap	*Pholiota aurivella*	uncommon
____	Scaly Pholiota	*Pholiota squarrosa*	uncommon
____	Sharp-scaly Pholiota	*Pholiota squarrosoides*	common
____	Dung-loving Psilocybe	*Psilocybe coprophila*	occasional
____	Wine-cap Stropharia	*Stropharia rugosoannulata*	fairly common

TRICHOLOMA FAMILY – Tricholomataceae [19]

____	Honey Mushroom	*Armillaria (Armillariella) mellea*	uncommon
____	Ringless Honey Mushroom	*Armillaria (Armillariella) tabescens*	uncommon
____	Funnel Clitocybe / Forest Funnelcap	*Clitocybe gibba*	common
____	Blewit	*Clitocybe nuda*	fairly common
____	Fat-footed Clitocybe / Clubfoot	*Clitocybe clavipes*	common
____	Little Brown Collybia	*Collybia alkalivirens*	occasional
____	Velvet Foot	*Flammulina velutipes*	fairly common
____	Common Laccaria	*Laccaria laccata*	fairly common
____	Purple-gilled Laccaria	*Laccaria ochropurpurea*	fairly common
____	Fairy Ring Mushroom	*Marasmius oreades*	common
____	Pinwheel Marasmius	*Marasmius rotula*	common
____	Orange Pinwheel Marasmius	*Marasmius siccus*	fairly common
____	Jack O'Lantern	*Omphalotus olearius*	fairly common
____	Late Fall Oyster	*Panellus serotinus*	fairly common
____	Veiled Oyster	*Pleurotus dryinus*	uncommon
____	Oyster Mushroom	*Pleurotus ostreatus*	occasional
____	Platterful Mushroom	*Megacollybia (Tricholomopsis) platyphylla*	fairly common
____	Orange Mycena	*Mycena leaiana*	common
____	Dark Gray Trich	*Tricholoma terreum*	fairly common

County Status Codes:

Common	routinely encountered – these are found rather easily
Fairly Common	a familiar fern or ally; should be found by the seeker
Uncommon	sporadically found; usually requires an effort to locate
Occasional	often difficult to find; a lot of searching . . . or you may get lucky!
Rare	will likely require an extensive search over a period of time

g	found only in the gametophyte stage (2)
e	endangered or threatened species (or potentially so) in Pennsylvania (1)

Latin and common nomenclature follows Rhoads and Block (see **Sources**). To facilitate use of the widespread *Peterson Guide to Ferns* (Cobb) in identifying species, parentheses surround common names used in Cobb's guide wherever there is sufficient difference in both common and scientific names to confuse the reader. Also, go to *Ferns & Fern Allies* at bhort.bh.cornell.edu/fern-cf.htm#diphasiastrum to learn some of the alternate names; helpful synonymy is listed there. A field guide devoted to the ferns & allies of Pennsylvania (J. Parks and J. Montgomery) is in progress and will be available within a year or two. Varieties, forms, and hybrids are mostly ignored in the summary below.

Species: [51] Additions are likely, but relatively few.

Class Equisetinae

HORSETAIL FAMILY – Equisetaceae [3]   **Status**

____	**Field Horsetail**	*Equisetum arvense*	fairly common
____	**Water (or Swamp) Horsetail**	*Equisetum fluviatile*	rare
____	**Woodland Horsetail**	*Equisetum sylvaticum*	occasional

Class Isoetinae

QUILLWORT FAMILY – Isoetaceae [1]

____	**Engelmann's Quillwort**	*Isoetes englemannii*	occasional

Class Lycopodiinae

CLUBMOSS FAMILY – Lycopodiaceae [9]

____	**Running-Pine** (Running Pine)	*Diphasiastrum digitatum*	fairly common
____	**Deep-rooted Running-Pine** (Ground Cedar)	*Diphasiastrum tristachyum*	fairly common
____	**Shining Firmoss** (Shining Clubmoss)	*Huperzia lucidulua*	common
____	**Northern Bog Clubmoss** (Bog Clubmoss)	*Lycopodiella inundata*	rare
____	**Bristly Clubmoss** (Stiff Clubmoss)	*Lycopodium annotinum*	fairly common
____	**Common Clubmoss** (Staghorn Clubmoss)	*Lycopodium clavatum*	fairly common
____	**Round-branched Ground-Pine**	*Lycopodium dendroideum*	uncommon
____	**Hickey's Ground-Pine**	*Lycopodium hickeyi*	rare
____	**Flat-branched Ground-Pine** (Tree Clubmoss)	*Lycopodium obscurum*	common

Class Filicinae

Order Ophioglossales – Succulent Ferns

SUCCULENT FERN FAMILY – Ophioglossaceae [5]

____	**Cut-leaved Grape Fern**	*Botrychium dissectum v. dissectum*	fairly common
		v. obliquum	fairly common
____	**Triangle Moonwort**	*Botrychium lanceolatum*	rare
____	**Daisy-leaved Moonwort**	*Botrychium matricariaefolium*	occasional
____	**Rattlesnake Fern**	*Botrychium virginianum*	common
____	**Blunt-lobed Grape Fern**	*Botrychium oneidense*	rare

FERNS & ALLIES of Somerset County, PA

Order Eufilicales –True Ferns [33]
The familial taxonomy below this level is currently under debate and therefore not included.

"ROYAL" FERNS		Status
Interrupted Fern	*Osmunda claytoniana*	common
Cinnamon Fern	*Osmunda cinnamomea*	common
Royal Fern	*Osmunda regalis*	occasional

OTHER FERNS		
Northern Maidenhair / Maidenhair Fern	*Adiantum pedatum*	fairly common
Mountain Spleenwort	*Asplenium montanum*	rare
Ebony Spleenwort	*Asplenium platyneuron*	common
Walking Fern	*Asplenium rhizophyllum*	occasional
Maidenhair Spleenwort	*Asplenium trichomanes*	uncommon
Lady Fern	*Athyrium filix-femina*	
"*Northern*"	*var. angustum*	common
"*Southern*"	*var. asplenoides*	fairly common
Fragile Fern	**Cystopteris tenuis*	uncommon
Hay-scented Fern	*Dennstaedtia punctilobula*	common
Silvery Glade Fern (S.Spleenwort)	*Deparia acrostichoides*	uncommon
Narrow-leaved Glade Fern (N-l Spleenwort)	*Diplazium pycnocarpon*	rare
Spinulose Wood Fern	*Dryopteris carthusiana*	common
Crested Wood Fern	*Dryopteris cristata*	uncommon
Goldie's Wood Fern	*Dryopteris goldiana*	uncommon
Evergreen Wood Fern	*Dryopteris intermedia*	common
Marginal Wood Fern	*Dryopteris marginalis*	common
Common Oak Fern	*Gymnocarpium dryopteris*	occasional
Ostrich Fern	*Matteucia struthiopteris*	occasional
Sensitive (or **Bead**) **Fern**	*Onoclea sensibilis*	common
Long Beech Fern	*Phegopteris connectilis*	rare
Broad Beech Fern	*Phegopteris hexagonoptera*	occasional
Appalachian Polypody	*Polypodium appalachianum*	fairly common
Common Polypody	*Polypodium virginianum*	common
Christmas Fern	*Polystichum acrostichoides*	common
Northern Bracken Fern	*Pteridium aquilinum v. latiusculum*	common
New York Fern	*Thelypteris noveboracensis*	common
Marsh Fern	*Thelypteris palustris*	uncommon
Rusty Woodsia	*Woodsia ilvensis*	rare
Blunt-lobed Woodsia	*Woodsia obtusa*	occasional
_g,e_ **Appalachian Grass Fern**	*Vittaria appalachiana*	rare
_g_ **Filmy Fern**	*Trichomanes intricatum*	rare

Most texts list *Cystopteris fragilis* as the species of **fragile fern for southern Pennsylvania, but fieldwork conducted by Dr. James Parks indicates that all collected specimens are actually attributed to *Cystopteris tenuis* (pers. com.).

Reviewed by:
James C. Parks, Ph.D. – Dept. of Biology, Millersville University, Millersville, PA

Sources:

Cobb, Boughton. 1963. *A Field Guide To The Ferns*. Houghton Mifflin Co., Boston. 281 pp.

Mickel, John T. 1979. *How to Know the Ferns and Fern Allies*. Wm. C. Brown Co, Dubuque. 229 pp.

Parks, James C. 1989. *Distribution of Gametophytic Populations of Vittaria and Trichomanes in Pennsylvania*. Rhodora 91:201-206.

Rhoads, Ann F., and Timothy A. Block. 2000. *The Plants of Pennsylvania, an Illustrated Manual*. University of Pennsylvania Press, Philadelphia. 1061 pp.

Rhoads, Ann F., and William M Klein, Jr. 1993. *The Vascular Flora of Pennsylvania Annotated Checklist and Atlas*. American Philosophical Society, Philadelphia. 636 pp.

Wherry, Edgar T. 1961. *The Fern Guide*. Doubleday & Co., Garden City, NY. 318 pp.

Wherry, Edgar T., John M. Fogg, and Herbert A. Wahl. 1979. *Atlas of the Flora of Pennsylvania*. The Morris Arboretum of the University of Pennsylvania, Philadelphia. 390 pp.

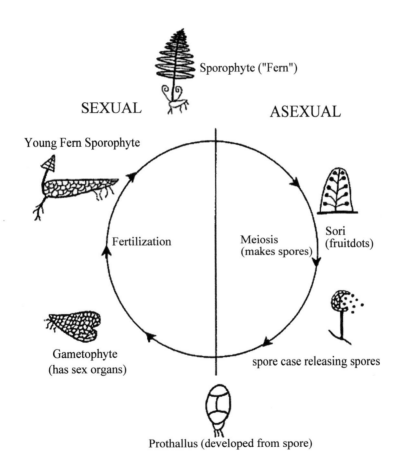

Figure 3 – Fern Life Cycle

Quotes of Note

John Muir:
It is always sunrise somewhere; the dew is never all dried at once; a shower is forever falling; vapor is forever rising.

Shakespeare:
One touch of nature makes the whole world kin.

Aristotle:
Nature does nothing uselessly.

Roger Tory Peterson:
In a world that seems so very puzzling is it any wonder birds have such appeal? Birds are, perhaps, the most eloquent expression of reality.

John Denver: *Rocky Mountain High*
Now he walks in quiet solitude, the forests and the streams
Seeking grace in every step he takes
His sight has turned inside himself to try and understand
The serenity of a clear blue mountain lake.

C.S. Lewis:
Because God created the Natural – invented it out of His love and artistry – it demands our reverence.

John James Audubon:
The woods would be very silent if no birds sang there except those who sing best.

Charles Dickens:
Nature gives to every time and season, some beauties of its own.

American Indian saying:
A pine needle fell in the forest:
The eagle saw it
The deer heard it
The bear smelled it.

General:

The student of nature does not usually turn first to the grasses, sedges, or rushes for excitement. But the grasses, sedges, and rushes are an important group. Plus, they are far more interesting than a quick glance would reveal. Learning these plants can be challenging, as we have many similar species. One reward is that it doesn't take long to know more than most everyone else! Worldwide, there are roughly 10,000 species of grass (102 here), 4000 species of sedge (86 here), and only 400 species of rush (14 here).

In many ways, the grasses support human life – ask a farmer about how this is so. Grasses include the **wheat, rye, corn,** and **rice** that feed us directly in the form of flour, bread, and pasta. Hybrid corn produces fantastically high yields versus wild types, and its development is a keystone achievement of modern agriculture. Also, **timothy hay, canary grass,** and other pasture grasses fuel our livestock to produce meat, milk, cheese, and eggs. Depending heavily upon grasses for a living, farmers are often good sources for learning some of the common species around a farm.

Most folks do not usually think of grasses, sedges, and rushes as flowering plants but they do indeed have pretty flowers – just very small ones. Because the flowering parts of these plants are so small, anyone learning them must be particularly diligent and persistent: it's not a game for the easily frustrated. In fact, for an accurate identification, many sedges require the expertise of a trained botanist. One commonly found type that is easily identified is the **yellow nut sedge.** This stout sedge grows in slightly wet spots and is easily recognized as it is considered a weed in gardens and tilled edges of cornfields.

Grasses, sedges, and rushes are all monocots, or one-seed-leaved plants. Comparisons between monocots and dicots are discussed more in the *Wildflowers* chapter.

One of our grasses has a special appeal. By late May, the pleasantly pungent fragrance of **sweet vernal grass** fills the country air where it grows. The scent of this common grass can be detected on dogs and cats that have run through it, as well as on peoples' pant legs. It is to be "smelled for" around the same time that **lilacs** grace the breeze. I often pick handfuls of **sweet vernal grass** to save for the remainder of the year as its bloom passes too quickly: it is not very aromatic by late June.

Where & When:

Grasses, sedges, and rushes may be found the year around but summer is naturally the best season for the most species. Some species are found in bloom early in the spring and others not until early autumn. Sedges and rushes are best identified after late summer when they fruit. Try looking in soils with differing amounts of moisture, protection, and shade in order to find different species. Planted lawn grasses are usually confusing in that they are laboratory hybrid products, but they can sometimes be identified with patience. Old lawns not chemically treated will welcome back native grasses over time.

A number of grasses, many sedges, and most rushes prefer wet places. Look for those species in shallow ponds, wet fields, swamps and streamside. The tufts or clumps of vegetation that are often seen in wet areas or shallow ponds are usually rushes. Some sedges also form clumps: **spikerushes** (which are sedges) resemble little clusters of lions' tails, and they prefer standing water.

Facts & Figures:

➤ Grasses cover ⅓ of the earth's land surface and ½ of the United States.
➤ Grasses represent a major food source that includes wheat, rye, corn, rice, oats, and sugar.
➤ The Poaceae (grass family) has the third largest number of species worldwide after the Orchidaceae (orchids – of all things!) and Asteraceae (daisies, et al.).
➤ **Timothy** grass is named for a farmer, Timothy Hanson, who first suggested its use for crop hay in 1720.
➤ If you find a plant with a triangular stem, it is likely a sedge.
➤ In most plants, growth occurs at the top of the leaf or shoot. Grass growth is from the bottom which explains why lawns must be mowed.
➤ In our area, grasslands are not permanent, but would eventually return to forests if left alone. Permanent, or end-stage, grasslands are found in the mid-west of the United States.
➤ **Pediceled woolgrass** *(Scirpus pedicellatus)* reaches its southernmost limit, east of Laurel Mountain, in Somerset County.
➤ Ruminants such as cows and deer can digest grass leaves (cellulose) – humans can digest only the grains.
➤ **Soft rush** *(Juncus effusus)* is sometimes used for matting and in chair bottoms.
➤ The only collection of **smallfruit spikerush** *(Eleocharis microcarpa)* from Pennsylvania was from Somerset County in 1898.

Some Terms of Interest:

Achene fruit of the *sedge* family (along with some other families)

Capsule fruit of the *rush* family (along with some other families)

Grain fruit of the *grass* family

Grass a family of flowering plants: narrow leaves with parallel veins, small flowers with specialized structures, and round – mostly hollow – stems except at joints

Hay usually refers to grasses, but also forbs (herbs other than grasses) like alfalfa cut and dried for feed

Joint found on grasses, but not sedges/rushes; also called nodes – where leaves are attached to the stem

Rushes similar to grasses and sedges but distinguished by flower structure that is similar to, but smaller than that of a lily

Sedge stems mostly triangular and solid, closed sheath *vs.* open sheath of grasses

Sheath part of the leaf that wraps around the stem

Silage grasses and legumes are chopped and blown into an airtight silo to form fermented feed

Sod surface of the ground consisting of grasses, their roots, and soil

Straw stalks of grain (e.g., oats) gathered after the grain is harvested; then used for animal bedding

Weed any plant growing where it is not wanted

Activities:

- On the chapter list, check all of the plants that you have found. Make notes on where and when.
- The next time you eat corn-on-the-cob, remember that you are eating grass fruits.
- without feeling the need to assign a name to them, take a half hour's summer walk through fields and thickets and check out all the various types of grasses there; you'll probably be surprised by the variety.
- Try to avoid the manicured greens that have become the pride of suburban America. A monochromatic grass is largely sterile and devoid of interesting "stuff." Pumping herbicides onto your lawn ensures that the diversity of mushrooms, birds, beetles, small flora, toads, salamanders, et al., will have to live somewhere else; the absence of this exciting array of life creates a dull space. A **dandelion** carpet doesn't last that long and is rather pretty during its short May life.
- Read accounts of the prairie in books like Laura Ingalls Wilder's *Little House* series. That's about as close as you'll get these days as the immense **tall-grass prairies** of pioneer days have now become roughly the *Corn Belt*, the richest soil on earth. Precious little of that habitat remains – but it still can be found around the Flint Hills region of Kansas and also along railroad right-of-ways in the Midwest. **Short-grass prairies** have fared only slightly better, much of it becoming what is now the *Wheat Belt*.
- Grasses, sedges, and rushes may be researched at plants.usda.gov/plants/cgi_bin/topics.cgi.
- See for yourself that grasses, sedges and rushes are families of flowering plants: look closely at **timothy** hay to note the purplish blooms found on the heads.
- If you own enough land, let a small section of your lawn go untended for five years to see the change.
- Watch along the turnpike for the very tall "phrag" *(Phragmites australis)* that towers over your head to fifteen feet! Another lofty grass that you may find, at nine feet, is **Indian grass** *(Sorghastrum nutans)*.

County Status Codes:

common	widespread and easy to find in most of the county
uncommon	a bit harder to find and an effort sometimes needed; locally common
occasional	infrequently found; scattered occurrence; may be locally common
rare	difficult to locate; extensive search may fail
a	alien species, not native to Pennsylvania (35)
e	endangered or threatened species (or potentially so) in Pennsylvania (11)

Common names for these plants vary widely from one source to another and are frequently unreliable. As this is the case, be sure to pinpoint identifications based on the Latin nomenclature. The common names used here were taken from multiple sources. The Latin names are those found in Rhoads & Block (see **Sources**). Some alternate scientific names used in various recent references are noted in parentheses.

Species: [202] Additions are likely, but relatively few.

RUSH FAMILY – Juncaceae [14]   **Status**

____	Sharp-fruited Rush	*Juncus acuminatus*	common
____ e	Smallhead Rush	*Juncus brachycephalus*	occasional
____	Narrow-panicled Rush	*Juncus brevicaudatus*	rare
____	Toad Rush	*Juncus bufonius*	occasional
____	Canada Rush	*Juncus canadensis*	occasional
____	Soft Rush	*Juncus effusus*	common
____	Blackfoot Rush	*Juncus gerardii*	rare
____	Grass-leaved Rush	*Juncus marginatus*	uncommon
____	Woodland Rush	*Juncus subcaudatus*	occasional
____	Poverty (or **Yard** or **Path**) Rush	*Juncus tenuis*	common
____	Carolina Woodrush	*Luzula acuminata*	common
____ e	Bulbous Woodrush	*Luzula bulbosa*	rare
____	Hedgehog Woodrush	*Luzula echinata*	rare
____	Common (or **Field**) Woodrush	*Luzula multiflora*	common

SEDGE FAMILY – Cyperaceae [86]

____	Densetuft Hairsedge / Sand-Rush	*Bulbostylis capillaris*	uncommon
____	Summer Sedge	*Carex aestivalis*	rare
____	Whitetinge Sedge	*Carex albicans*	uncommon
____	White Bear Sedge	*Carex albursina*	rare
____	Eastern Narrowleaf Sedge	*Carex amphibola*	rare
____	Yellowfruit Sedge	*Carex annectens*	occasional
____	Appalachian Sedge	*Carex appalachica*	occasional
____	Hay Sedge	*Carex argyrantha*	uncommon
____	Bog Sedge	*Carex atlantica*	uncommon
____	Bailey's Sedge	*Carex baileyi*	common
____	Eastern Woodland Sedge	*Carex blanda*	rare
____	Bromelike Sedge	*Carex bromoides*	uncommon
____	Brownish Sedge	*Carex brunnescens*	occasional
____	Bush's Sedge	*Carex bushii*	occasional
____	Silvery Sedge	*Carex canescens*	occasional
____	Oval-leaf Sedge	*Carex cephalophora*	common
____	Fibrousroot Sedge	*Carex communis*	common
____	Soft Fox Sedge	*Carex conjuncta*	rare
____ e	Short Hair Sedge	*Carex crinita*	occasional
____	White Edge Sedge	*Carex debilis*	uncommon
____	Slender Woodland Sedge	*Carex digitalis*	occasional
____	Prickly Sedge	*Carex echinata*	uncommon
____	Emmons' Sedge	*Carex emmonsii*	rare
____	Northern Long Sedge	*Carex folliculata*	common
____	Frank's Sedge	*Carex frankii*	occasional
____	Slender Looseflower Sedge	*Carex gracilescens*	occasional
____	Graceful Sedge	*Carex gracillima*	occasional
____	Nodding Sedge	*Carex gynandra*	common
____	Fuzzy Wuzzy Sedge	*Carex hirsutella*	occasional
____	Pubescent Sedge	*Carex hirtifolia*	rare
____	Greater Bladder Sedge	*Carex intumescens*	common
____	Spreading Sedge	*Carex laxiculmis*	occasional
____	Broad Looseflower Sedge	*Carex laxiflora*	common
____	Bristlystalked Sedge	*Carex leptalea*	uncommon
____	Nerveless Woodland Sedge	*Carex leptonervia*	uncommon

SEDGE FAMILY – continued

			Status
____	Blue Ridge Sedge	*Carex lucorum*	rare
____ e	False Hop Sedge	*Carex lupuliformis*	rare
____	Hop Sedge	*Carex lupulina*	uncommon
____	Shallow Sedge	*Carex lurida*	common
____	Black Edge Sedge	*Carex nigromarginata*	rare
____	Greater Straw Sedge	*Carex normalis*	uncommon
____	Longstalk Sedge	*Carex pedunculata*	rare
____	Pennsylvania Sedge	*Carex pensylvanica*	common
____	Plantain Sedge	*Carex plantaginea*	occasional
____	Broad-leaf Sedge	*Carex platyphylla*	occasional
____	Drooping Sedge	*Carex prasina*	uncommon
____	Necklace Sedge	*Carex projecta*	rare
____	Eastern Star Sedge	*Carex radiata*	common
____	Rosy Sedge	*Carex rosea*	occasional
____	Eastern Rough Sedge	*Carex scabrata*	uncommon
____	Broom Sedge	*Carex scoparia*	uncommon
____	Burr Reed Sedge	*Carex sparganioides*	occasional
____	Squarrose Sedge	*Carex squarrosa*	rare
____	Owlfruit Sedge	*Carex stipata*	common
____	Tussock Sedge	*Carex stricta*	uncommon
____	Swan's Sedge	*Carex swanii*	occasional
____	Quill Sedge	*Carex tenera*	rare
____	Twisted Sedge	*Carex torta*	uncommon
____	Blunt Broom Sedge	*Carex tribuloides*	occasional
____	Three-seeded Sedge	*Carex trisperma*	occasional
____	Northwest Territory Sedge	*Carex utriculata*	occasional
____	Fox Sedge	*Carex vulpinoidea*	common
____	Willdenow's Sedge	*Carex willdenovii*	rare
____	Pretty Sedge	*Carex woodii*	uncommon
____ e	Fraser's Cymophyllus	*Cymophyllus fraserianus*	rare
____	Shining Cyperus	*Cyperus bipartitus (rivularis)*	uncommon
____	Yellow Nut Sedge	*Cyperus esculentus*	common
____	Yellow Flatsedge	*Cyperus flavescens*	uncommon
____	Strawcolored Flatsedge	*Cyperus strigosus*	uncommon
____	Threeway Sedge	*Dulichium arundinaceum*	uncommon
____	Needle Spikerush	*Eleocharis acicularis*	uncommon
____	Bald Spikerush	*Eleocharis erythropoda*	rare
____	Smallfruit Spikerush	*Eleocharis microcarpa*	rare
____	Blunt Spikerush	*Eleocharis obtusa*	common
____	Slender Spikerush	*Eleocharis tenuis*	common
____	Tawny Cottongrass	*Eriophorum virginicum*	uncommon
____ e	Thinleaf Cottonsedge	*Eriophorum viridicarinatum*	rare
____	White Beaksedge	*Rhynchospora alba*	rare
____	Brownish Beaksedge	*Rhynchospora capitellata*	occasional
____	Great Bulrush	*Schoenoplectus tabernaemontani (Scirpus validus)*	uncommon
____	Dark Green Bulrush	*Scirpus atrovirens*	common
____	Woolgrass	*Scirpus cyperinus*	common
____	Georgia Bulrush	*Scirpus georgianus*	rare
____	Mosquito Bulrush	*Scirpus hattorianus*	common
____ e	Pediceled Woolgrass	*Scirpus pedicellatus*	rare
____	Leafy Bulrush	*Scirpus polyphyllus*	uncommon

GRASS FAMILY – Poaceae (also Gramineae) [102]

			Status
____	a	Redtop	*Agrostis gigantea (alba)*	common
____		Upland Bent	*Agrostis perennans*	common
____		Ticklegrass	*Agrostis scabra*	uncommon
____	a	Creeping Bent Grass	*Agrostis stolonifera (palustris)*	uncommon
____		Big Bluestem	*Andropogon gerardii*	uncommon
____	e	Bushy Bluestem / Broomsedge	*Andropogon glomeratus*	rare
____		Broomsedge	*Andropogon virginicus*	rare
____	a	Sweet Vernal Grass	*Anthoxanthum aristatum*	rare
____	a	Sweet Vernal Grass	*Anthoxanthum odoratum*	common
____		Poverty Grass	*Aristida dichotoma*	common
____	a	Tall Oatgrass	*Arrhenatherum elatius*	common
____		Long-awned Wood Grass	*Brachyelytrum erectum*	common
____	a	Field Chess	*Bromus arvensis*	rare
____	a	Fringed Brome Grass	*Bromus ciliatus*	rare
____	a	Common Hairy Chess	*Bromus commutatus*	uncommon
____	a	Smooth Brome	*Bromus inermis*	common
____	a	Japanese Chess	*Bromus japonicus*	rare
____		Brome Grass / Canada Brome	*Bromus pubescens*	uncommon
____	a	Common Smooth Chess	*Bromus secalinus*	occasional
____		Blue Joint	*Calamagrostis canadensis*	uncommon
____		Reedgrass	*Calamagrostis cinnoides*	occasional
____		Sweet Woodreed / Wood Reedgrass	*Cinna arundinacea*	common
____		Drooping Woodreed	*Cinna latifolia*	rare
____	a	Orchard Grass	*Dactylis glomerata*	common
____		Flattened Oatgrass	*Danthonia compressa*	uncommon
____		Poverty Oatgrass	*Danthonia spicata*	common
____	a	Smooth Crab Grass	*Digitaria ischaemum*	common
____	a	Hairy Crab Grass	*Digitaria sanguinalis*	common
____	a	Barnyard Grass	*Echinochloa crusgalli*	common
____		Barnyard Grass	*Echinochloa muricata (pungens)*	common
____		Bottlebrush Grass	*Elymus (Hystrix) patula*	uncommon
____		Riverbank Wild Rye	*Elymus riparius*	uncommon
____		Slender Wheatgrass	*Elymus trachycaulus (Agropyron trachycaulum)*	rare
____		Hairy Wild Rye	*Elymus villosus*	occasional
____		Virginia Wild Rye	*Elymus virginicus*	common
____	a	Quack Grass	*Elytrigia (Agropyron) repens*	common
____		Lacegrass	*Eragrostis capillaris*	occasional
____		Teal (or Creeping) Lovegrass	*Eragrostis hypnoides*	occasional
____		Tufted (or Carolina) Lovegrass	*Eragrostis pectinacea*	uncommon
____	a	Indian Lovegrass	*Eragrostis pilosa*	rare
____	a	Fescue	*Festuca elatior*	uncommon
____		Nodding Fescue	*Festuca obtusa*	common
____	a	Meadow Ryegrass / Meadow Fescue	*Festuca pratensis*	common
____		Rattlesnake Mannagrass	*Glyceria canadensis*	uncommon
____		American Mannagrass	*Glyceria grandis*	occasional
____		Melic (or Slender) Mannagrass	*Glyceria melicaria*	common
____	e	Coastal (or Blunt) Mannagrass	*Glyceria obtusa*	rare
____		Floating Mannagrass	*Glyceria septentrionalis*	uncommon
____		Fowl Mannagrass	*Glyceria striata*	common
____	a	Velvet Grass	*Holcus lanatus*	common
____		Rice Cutgrass	*Leersia oryzoides*	common
____		Whitegrass	*Leersia virginica*	common
____	a	Sprangletop	*Leptochloa fascicularis*	rare
____	a	English (or Perennial) Ryegrass	*Lolium perenne*	occasional

GRASS FAMILY – continued

			Status
____e	**Three-flowered Melic**	*Melica nitens*	rare
____a	**Millet Grass**	*Milium effusum*	uncommon
____	**Wirestem Muhly**	*Muhlenbergia frondosa*	uncommon
____	**Nimblewill / Dropseed**	*Muhlenbergia schreberi*	uncommon
____	**Woodland Muhly**	*Muhlenbergia sylvatica*	uncommon
____e	**Fall Dropseed Muhly**	*Muhlenbergia uniflora*	rare
____	**Mountain Rice / Spreading Ricegrass**	*Oryzopsis asperifolia*	occasional
____	**Blackseed Ricegrass**	*Oryzopsis racemosa*	rare
____	**Western Panicgrass**	*Panicum acuminatum (implicatum)*	common
____	**Bosc's Panicgrass**	*Panicum boscii*	rare
____	**Old Witch Grass**	*Panicum capillare*	common
____	**Deer-tongue Grass**	*Panicum clandestinum*	common
____	**Fall Panicum**	*Panicum dichotomiflorum*	uncommon
____	**Cypress Panicgrass**	*Panicum dichotomum*	uncommon
____	**Gattinger's Panicgrass**	*Panicum gattingeri*	common
____	**Broad-leaved Panicgrass**	*Panicum latifolium*	common
____	**Slimleaf Panicgrass**	*Panicum linearifolium*	occasional
____	**Matting Rosette Grass**	*Panicum meridonale*	rare
____	**Roundseed Panicgrass**	*Panicum microcarpon*	uncommon
____	**Woodland Witchgrass**	*Panicum philadelphicum*	occasional
____	**Redtop Panicgrass**	*Panicum rigidulum (agrostoides)*	uncommon
____	**Redtop Panicgrass**	*Panicum stipitatum*	occasional
____	**Switch Grass**	*Panicum virgatum*	uncommon
____	**Reed Canary Grass**	*Phalaris arundinacea*	common
____a	**Timothy**	*Phleum pratense*	common
____	**Common Reed / "Phrag"**	*Phragmites australis (communis)*	occasional
____	**Grove Bluegrass**	*Poa alsodes*	common
____a	**Low Speargrass / Annual Bluegrass**	*Poa annua*	uncommon
____a	**Canada Bluegrass**	*Poa compressa*	common
____	**Early Bluegrass**	*Poa cuspidata*	uncommon
____a	**Kentucky Bluegrass**	*Poa pratensis*	common
____	**Oldpasture Bluegrass**	*Poa saltuensis*	uncommon
____a	**Rough Bluegrass**	*Poa trivialis*	uncommon
____a	**Alkali Grass / Goosegrass**	*Puccinellia distans*	rare
____	**Purple Oat**	*Schizachne purpurascens*	rare
____	**Little Bluestem**	*Schizachyrium scoparium (Andropogon scoparius)*	occasional
____a	**Rye**	*Secale cereale*	occasional
____a	**Giant Foxtail**	*Setaria faberi*	uncommon
____a	**Yellow Foxtail**	*Setaria pumila (lutescens)*	uncommon
____a	**Green Foxtail**	*Setaria viridis*	uncommon
____	**Indian Grass**	*Sorghastrum nutans*	uncommon
____a	**Johnson Grass**	*Sorghum halepense*	uncommon
____	**Shiny Wedgescale**	*Sphenopholis nitida*	uncommon
____	**Slender Wedgescale**	*Sphenopholis obtusata (intermedia)*	uncommon
____	**Poverty Grass**	*Sporobolus vaginiflorus*	uncommon
____	**False Mannagrass / Pale Meadowgrass**	*Torryeochloa (Puccinellia) pallida*	occasional
____	**Purpletop Tridens**	*Tridens flavus*	uncommon
____a	**Foxtail Fescue**	*Vulpina myuros*	rare

Reviewed by:

Carl S. Keener, Ph.D. – Professor Emeritus of Biology, The Pennsylvania State University

Sources:

Brown, Lauren. 1979. *Grasses, An Identification Guide.* Houghton Mifflin Co., Boston. 240 pp.

Jennings, O.E. 1953. *Wildflowers of Western Pennsylvania and The Upper Ohio Basin* Vol. I University of Pittsburgh Press, Pittsburgh. 574 pp.

Knobel, Edward. 1980. *Field Guide to the Grasses, Sedges and Rushes of the United States.* Dover Publications, Inc., New York. 83 pp.

Rhoads, Ann F., and Timothy A. Block. 2000. *The Plants of Pennsylvania, An Illustrated Manual.* University of Pennsylvania Press, Philadelphia. 1061 pp.

Rhoads, Ann F., and William M Klein, Jr. 1993. *The Vascular Flora of Pennsylvania: Annotated Checklist and Atlas.* American Philosophical Society, Philadelphia. 636 pp.

USDA, NRCS. 1999. The PLANTS database (http://plants.usda.gov/plants). National Plant Data Center, Baton Rouge, LA. 70874-4490 USA.

Wherry, Edgar T., John M. Fogg, and Herbert A. Wahl. 1979. *Atlas of the Flora of Pennsylvania.* The Morris Arboretum of the University of Pennsylvania, Philadelphia. 390 pp.

▶ Remember that it is illegal to collect any flora or fauna in state and national parks.

FLOWERING PLANT FAMILY INDEX

The large number of flowering plants comprising the grasses through the trees (the Class Angiospermae or Magnoliophyta) are divided artificially into three chapters here: grasses/sedges/rushes, wildflowers, and trees/shrubs. Some families are represented in two of these chapters. That state of affairs, along with most peoples' unfamiliarity with the phylogenetic order of appearance, may pose a little difficulty in quickly locating a given family in those chapters. This index is provided to assist in finding page numbers for families of flowering plants.

WILDFLOWERS of Somerset County, PA

General:

The term *wildflowers* is mildly ambiguous. Most of our woody and herbaceous (non-woody) plants produce flowers, but neither maple trees nor panicgrasses are thought of as wildflowers. Distinctions between wildflowers and grasses or trees are occasionally arbitrary or misleading. For example, clovers are much more closely related to **black locust** trees than they are to violets. Clover and locust are both, in fact, in the same family called Fabaceae. But many people think of clovers and violets as being more alike since they're both considered wildflowers. Additional uncertainty lies in the regular occurrence of domestic flowers growing "wild" and wildflowers being cultivated. However, it is not that important to form a concrete distinction and the plants included here mostly follow the general meaning of the term: non-woody plants which flower and grow apart from cultivation (grasses, sedges, and rushes excepted).

There is no ambiguity about the *appeal* of wildflowers – they add a glorious array of color to the world about us. From orchid pinks to gentian blues to buttercup yellows, they are the rainbows of the wild floral community. Here in Somerset, outdoor enthusiasts eagerly anticipate the blooming of the first flowers of spring. **Coltsfoot** is often given credit for being the first bloomer and shows up along roadsides from mid to late March. But **skunk cabbage** actually has it beat, pushing blooms up through the snow in late February. In fact, during warmer periods through the winter, **dandelions** and **chickweeds** can sometimes be found taking advantage of these thaws by producing flowers, and later, seeds, thus aiding in the ongoing cycle of reproduction.

Learning the wildflowers is an easily assumed hobby. They're numerous in most habitat types and there are lots of books that discuss identification. Apart from technical keys, Peterson & McKenny's guide is the best visual-approach book for that purpose. There are enough wildflowers to guard against monotony and not so many as to make their familiarization tiresome. In early phases of study, so much time is spent cross-checking guides for names that one soon begins to recognize new flowers by name without consulting the texts.

Their beauty is justification enough for learning the wildflowers, but knowledge here may have other benefits as well. Wildflower lore can reveal facts about the soil type they're on, the moisture available, and the associated wildlife which should occur with them. And then, recognizing which plant species may be consumed in an emergency enhances wilderness survival skills. Also, perhaps, romance is heightened. The notion of picking wildflowers for a sweetheart is probably about as old as the notion of wildflowers. Potential suitors take heed: naming wildflowers at a glance is impressive knowledge.

The only collection of **saltmarsh sand-spurrey** in PA was from Somerset County in 1987 – due to extensive use of de-icing salt here. And we boast many other rarities: **Jacob's-ladder, bog aster, mountain goldenrod, whorled pogonia, pink lady's slipper** (white form), and **white monkshood** to name a few. Learn the common species by your home first; and then expand into local woods and fields.

Where & When:

The area within a mile or two of your home will contain the majority of the species listed in this chapter. As with all wildlife, varying the habitat types in your search will pay big dividends in numbers found. Some of the better known wildflowers are grouped by season here:

SPRING (March – May)

Skunk Cabbage	Toothworts	Trout Lily	Blue Phlox
Trailing Arbutus	Dutchman's Breeches	Ladyslipper	May-Apple
Trilliums	Violets	Marsh Marigold	Fringed Polygala
Hepatica	Wild Geranium	Jack-in-the-Pulpit	Bluets
Bloodroot	Spring Beauty	Wild Ginger	Columbine

SUMMER (June – August)

Buttercups	Wooly/Moth Mulleins	Bouncing Bet	Touch-Me-Not
Queen Anne's Lace	St. Johnsworts	Blue-eyed Grass	(Jewel-weeds)
Evening Primrose	Brown-eyed Susan	Butter-and-Eggs	White Baneberry
Poison Ivy	Day-Lily, Turk's-Cap	Black Cohosh	(Doll's Eyes)
Chicory	Lily, Tiger Lily	Yarrow	Cinquefoils
Orange Hawkweed	Bee Balm	Indian Pipe	Teasel

FALL (August – November)

Monkey Flower	Goldenrods	Woodland Sunflower	Gentians
Lobelias	Asters	Ironweed	Ladies'-Tresses
Cardinal Flower	Turtlehead	Joe-Pye-Weed	+ summer carry-overs

WILDFLOWERS of Somerset County, PA

Facts & Figures:

➤ Square-stemmed plants are likely to be members of the mint family.

➤ American Indians used leaf and root juices of **bloodroot** to paint their faces and teepees.

➤ Early medicine often employed plants that resembled the desired target organ (Doctrine of Signatures). In this manner, **liver leaf** that physically resembles lobes of a liver was used in treating suspected liver ailments and is known today as **Hepatica** (*hepatic* references liver) for that reason.

➤ The juice of leaves from crumbled **jewelweed,** also known as **touch-me-not,** may be rubbed as a balm on skin to sooth **poison ivy** or **itchweed** irritations.

➤ You may gain a bit of etymology (science of word origin) through wildflower study. For instance: "orchid" means *testes* and a study of the flowers reproductive structures reveals why the name was chosen. "Crypt" refers to hidden or secretive (*cryptic* message). Thus it is understood why *cryptorchid* refers to hidden testicles in any so affected animal whose testes have not descended.

➤ Sweet Clovers were responsible in the development of the rodent poison dicoumarin (Warfarin®). WARF stands for <u>W</u>I <u>A</u>lumni <u>R</u>esearch <u>F</u>oundation and it was at the University of Wisconsin that a farmer brought in a bucket of uncoagulated blood from a cow that had eaten a lot of **sweet clover.** Dicoumarin occurs in sweet clover and so the cow could not clot blood because of eating those plants.

➤ **Pitcher-plant** and **sundew** are carnivorous plants! They digest proteins of trapped insects/tiny animals.

➤ There are 87 families of plants represented in this section – including 763 species! But 210 of those are "alien" species (mostly introduced by activities of man) that aren't native to this area. They frequent roadsides and disturbed areas as they don't compete well with our native species on their own turf.

➤ The Greek philosopher Socrates was forced to commit suicide by consuming **poison hemlock** extract. This plant and the related **water hemlock** are <u>deadly</u>, so uproot them when found near home or farm.

➤ **Goldenrods** are frequently blamed for the fall allergy season, but the real culprit is mostly **ragweed.**

➤ **Queen-Anne's-lace** is the ancestor of our garden carrot and is often called wild carrot. The "black thing" at the center of the umbel, or flower cluster, is one or several dark florets.

➤ Garden tomatoes are in the Nightshade family, many of which have mildly poisonous fruits.

➤ Needles, thorns, and bitter taste are defense mechanisms whereby plants may avoid being eaten.

➤ When **asters** appear, summer is on the wane and autumn is right around the corner.

➤ Plants may have both female and male parts in the same flower, both parts in different flowers on the same plant, or some cases (e.g., the Holly family) in which a whole plant is either male or female.

Some Terms of Interest:

Angiosperms	any of the class Angiospermae with seeds in a closed ovary: simply . . . flowering plants
Alternate	leaves alternate from one side to the other along the stalk: one leaf per node
Opposite	leaves are opposite each other along the stalk; two leaves per node
Whorled	three or more leaves (or flowers) from one node along a stem
Lanceolate	a leaf shape description; this one (of many) indicates longer than wide with a pointed end
Annual	any given plant species which completes the life cycle in one growing season
Biennial	any given plant species growing vegetatively the first year, fruiting and dying the second
Perennial	any given plant species persisting for at least several years with new herbaceous growth
Botanizing	equivalent of "birding" or "fishing"; to go out looking for interesting plant species
Cultivar	a <u>culti</u>vated <u>var</u>iety of a wild plant; e.g., greenhouse developed strain of bleeding heart
Monocot	subclass of Angiosperms: flower parts in 3's or multiples of 3, one seed leaf
Dicot	other subclass of Angiosperms: flower parts in 4's or 5's, two seed leaves
Emergent	aquatic vegetation with the base submerged and upper part extending out of the water
Pollination	the act of pollen being transferred from a *stamen* (male part) to a *pistil* (female part)
Glabrous	surface of a leaf or stem without hairs
Pubescent	one of many terms to describe hairiness of a plant – like wooly, downy, hirsute, etc.
Saprophyte	plant lacking chlorophyll – living off nutrients of <u>dead</u> organic matter (e.g., **Indian pipe**)
Parasite	plant lacking chlorophyll – gaining nutrients from <u>living</u> plants (e.g., **beechdrops**)
Calyx	collectively, the *sepals* of a flower; leaf-like structures usually beneath petals; usually green, but may be colored and resemble petals
Corolla	collectively, the *petals* of a flower; often brightly colored
Stamens	male flower parts; *pistils* = female flower parts (see figure 4 on page 64)
Weed	any plant growing where it is not wanted

WILDFLOWERS of Somerset County, PA

Activities:

- On the chapter list, check all of the wildflowers that you have found. Make notes on where and when.
- Blow **dandelion** seeds with your kids. Teach them to "pop" **jewelweed** seed cases in late summer or fall.
- Learn the edibles: **sheep sorrel** is abundant just about everywhere and puts a little zing in a salad.
- Note in each season when first and last representatives of a species are found in flower. Over a period of years you will begin to expect flowers to appear or fade away right before they do.
- Learn to identify **catnip;** find some and take it home to your cat – the effect on behavior is often bizarre.
- If you enjoy gardening, a wildflower garden enhances any back yard and will teach you plenty.
- The subject beauty, coupled with the lack of movement, makes wildflowers good photography subjects.
- Join the Botanical Society of Western Pennsylvania. Website: home.kiski.net/~speedy/b1.html
  Or contact them at The Botanical Society of W. PA, 5837 Nicholson Street, Pittsburgh, PA 15217.
- Pick a wildflower bouquet for someone special; be able to name the kinds of flowers picked. [*Never pick anything few in number or known to be uncommon to rare!*]
- Go to see **pitcher-plants** and **sundew** in the boggy glade by the Laurel Summit Picnic Area this summer (directions in **Appendix**). The bog is a short, easy hike from the picnic area.
- Learn the appropriate way to press plants so that they may be preserved in herbarium collections.
- Test to see if a child likes butter. Rub a dandelion on the back of their hand: yellow coloration = positive!
- Take a wildflower walk with a friend and see how many types you can find.
- Remember to learn the Latin names as part of your education – they'll often describe the plant or teach you something about it: **trillium** is from tril (three) and lium (leaf).
- Grow corn in one flat (shallow tray) and beans in another. Note that when the corn sprouts it has only one seed leaf (called a *cotyledon*) and when the beans sprout they have two seed leaves. Thus it is seen why there are monocots (mono=one) and dicots (di=two). There are many more dicot species than there are monocot species and that is reflected in their occurrences here in the county. Grasses (such as corn), sedges and rushes are all monocots.

County Status Codes:

These codes assume proper habitat, season, and reasonable effort during the course of a season. "Rare" species may be truly rare anywhere **(orchids),** rare overall but locally common **(sundew** in bogs), rare due to over-collection **(goldenseal),** rare due to being escapes from cultivation **(radish),** or rare due to being on the range fringe **(bladderwort).** A few may be common in nearby counties.

Abundant	easily found, perhaps in large numbers, throughout our area in season; can't miss
Common	usually found, either in smaller numbers or spotty distribution; won't miss
Fairly Common	not usually hard to find, may require a little effort; shouldn't miss
Uncommon	harder to find, may take a good effort but still turns up here and there; may miss
Occasional	rather difficult to find (or you may get lucky!); usually miss
Rare	very difficult to find; will miss most of the time
Very Rare	your chances of finding it unaided are roughly slim to none (and "Slim" just left town)
Extirpated?	it is presumed that the plant no longer occurs in Somerset County
Escape	escaped from cultivation, or similar situation; indicates scarce and not well naturalized

a = alien species not native to Pennsylvania (or often even the U.S.); either introduced or escaped (210)
e = endangered or threatened (or potentially so) in PA (41), *e✳* = Federal Endangered Species List (2)

Taxonomic nomenclature follows that found in Rhoads and Block (see **Sources**). Some alternate scientific names are listed in parentheses. Preference was often given here to the common names encountered in *Peterson's Field Guide*, since it is so widely used. As with all classes of organisms, there exists disagreement among taxonomists over nomenclature of various species of flowers – and most guidebooks do not list alternative scientific names. For those interested, consult the website maintained by the USDA for variations in nomenclature: plants.usda.gov. As for most chapters, families are listed in phylogenetic order below. Genus and species are listed alphabetically to facilitate locating a species listing within the text. When especially relevant, subspecies, varieties, and forms are noted.

WILDFLOWERS of Somerset County, PA

Species: [763] Additions are likely, but relatively few.

DICOTS (*subclass* of Angiosperms)

			Status
	WILD-GINGER FAMILY – Aristolochiaceae [2]		**Status**
____	**Virginia Snakeroot**	*Aristolochia serpentaria*	rare
____	**Wild Ginger**	*Asarum canadense*	uncommon

	WATERLILY FAMILY – Nymphaeaceae [1]		
____	**Spatterdock / Yellow Pond Lily**	*Nuphar lutea (advena)*	fairly common

	WATERSHIELD FAMILY – Cabombaceae [1]		
____	**Water-Shield**	*Brasenia schreberi*	occasional

BUTTERCUP FAMILY – Ranunculaceae [29]

____	*e*	**White Monkshood**	*Aconitum reclinatum*	very rare
____	*e*	**Monkshood**	*Aconitum uncinatum*	extirpated?
____		**White Baneberry / "Doll's Eyes"**	*Actaea pachypoda*	uncommon
	e	**Long-headed Thimbleweed** *(Anemone cylindrica)* mentioned in Jennings is probably erroneous		
____		**Wood Anemone**	*Anemone quinquefolia*	common
____		**Thimbleweed**	*Anemone virginiana*	fairly common
____		**Columbine**	*Aquilegia canadensis*	common
____	*a*	**European Columbine**	*Aquilegia vulgaris*	escape
____		**Marsh-Marigold / Cowslip**	*Caltha palustris*	fairly common

Former "Mountain Marsh-Marigold" *(Caltha palustris var. "flabellifolia")* has been attributed to the county but is no longer recognized as a valid form.

____	*e*	**American Bugbane**	*Cimicifuga americana*	uncommon
____		**Black Cohosh / Bugbane**	*Cimicifuga racemosa*	common
____		**Virgin's-Bower**	*Clematis virginiana*	fairly common
____		**Goldthread**	*Coptis trifolia (groenlandica)*	occasional
____		**Dwarf (or Spring) Larkspur**	*Delphinium tricorne*	very rare
____		**Sharp-lobed Hepatica / Liverleaf**	*Hepatica nobilis var. acuta*	fairly common
		Round-lobed Hepatica____	*Hepatica nobilis var. americana*	fairly common
____	*e*	**Goldenseal**	*Hydrastis canadensis*	rare
____		**Kidneyleaf Buttercup**	*Ranunculus abortivus*	common
____	*a*	**Common (or Tall) Buttercup**	*Ranunculus acris*	common
____		**Allegheny Buttercup**	*Ranunculus allegheniensis*	uncommon
____		**Spearwort**	*Ranunculus ambigens*	rare
____	*a*	**Bulbous Buttercup**	*Ranunculus bulbosus*	common
____		**Swamp Buttercup**	*Ranunculus caricetorum (septentrionalis)*	fairly common
____		**Hispid Buttercup**	*Ranunculus hispidus*	common
____		**Hooked Buttercup**	*Ranunculus recurvatus*	common
____	*a*	**Creeping Buttercup**	*Ranunculus repens*	common
____	*e*	**Maid of the Mist**	*Thalictrum coriaceum (incl. steeleanum)*	rare
____		**Early Meadow-Rue**	*Thalictrum dioicum*	uncommon
____		**Tall Meadow-Rue**	*Thalictrum pubescens (polygamum)*	fairly common
____		**Rue-Anemone**	*Thalictrum (Anemonella) thalictroides*	common
____	*e*	**False Bugbane / Carolina Tassel-Rue**	*Trautvetteria carolinensis*	very rare

BARBERRY FAMILY – Berberidaceae [3]

____	*a*	**Japanese Barberry**	*Berberis thunbergii*	fairly common
____		**Blue Cohosh**	*Caulophyllum thalictroides*	common
____		**May Apple**	*Podophyllum peltatum*	abundant

WILDFLOWERS of Somerset County, PA

			Status
MOONSEED FAMILY – Menispermaceae [1]			**Status**
____	Canada Moonseed	*Menispermum canadense*	rare
	POPPY FAMILY – Papaveraceae [3]		
____ *a*	Celandine	*Chelidonium majus*	fairly common
____ *a*	Opium Poppy	*Papaver somniferum*	escape
____	Bloodroot	*Sanguinaria canadensis*	uncommon
	FUMEROOT FAMILY – Fumariaceae [5]		
____	Allegheny-Vine / Climbing Fumitory	*Adlumia fungosa*	rare
____	Yellow Corydalis / Fumewort	*Corydalis flavula*	rare
____	Pale Corydalis	*Corydalis sempervirens*	fairly common
____	Squirrel-Corn	*Dicentra canadensis*	uncommon
____	Dutchman's-Breeches	*Dicentra cucullaria*	occasional
	HEMP FAMILY – Cannabaceae [2]		
____ *a*	Hemp / "Pot"	*Cannabis sativa*	escape
____	Hop	*Humulus lupulus*	rare
	NETTLE FAMILY – Urticaceae [5]		
____	False Nettle, Bog-Hemp	*Boehmeria cylindrica*	uncommon
____	Wood Nettle	*Laportea canadensis*	common
____	Pennsylvania Pellitory	*Parietaria pensylvanica*	rare
____	Clearweed	*Pilea pumila*	fairly common
____ *a*	Stinging Nettle	*Urtica dioica*	fairly common
	POKEWEED FAMILY – Phytolaccaceae [1]		
____	Pokeweed	*Phytolacca americana*	abundant
	GOOSEFOOT FAMILY – Chenopodiaceae [6]		
____	Halberd-leaved Orach	*Atriplex prostrata*	rare
____ *a*	Lamb's Quarters	*Chenopodium album*	abundant
____ *e*	Strawberry Blite	*Chenopodium capitatum*	very rare
____	Maple-leaved Goosefoot	*Chenopodium gigantospermum* (*hybridum*)	fairly common
____ *a*	Oak-leaved Goosefoot	*Chenopodium glaucum*	rare
____ *a*	Belvedere	*Kochia scoparia*	escape
	AMARANTH FAMILY – Amaranthaceae [2]		
____ *a*	Green Amaranth / Pigweed	*Amaranthus hybridus*	fairly common
____ *a*	Green Pigweed	*Amaranthus retroflexus*	abundant
	PURSLANE FAMILY – Portulaceae [3]		
____	Carolina Spring-Beauty	*Claytonia caroliniana*	uncommon
____	Spring-Beauty	*Claytonia virginica*	common
____ *a*	Purslane	*Portulaca oleracea*	fairly common
	CARPET-WEED FAMILY – Molluginaceae [1]		
____ *a*	Carpet-Weed / Indian Chickweed	*Mollugo verticillata*	uncommon
	PINK FAMILY – Caryophyllaceae [25]		
____ *a*	Corn-Cockle	*Agrostemma githago*	rare
____ *a*	Thyme-leaved Sandwort	*Arenaria serpyllifolia*	fairly common
____ *a*	Mouse-Ear Chickweed	*Cerastium fontanum* (*vulgatum*)	common
____ *a*	Mouse-Ear Chickweed	*Cerastium glomeratum*	occasional

WILDFLOWERS of Somerset County, PA

PINK FAMILY – continued

			Status
	Nodding Chickweed	*Cerastium nutans*	uncommon
a	Deptford Pink	*Dianthus armeria*	common
a	Bunch Pink / Sweet-William	*Dianthus barbatus*	escape
	Grove Sandwort	*Moehringia (Arenaria) lateriflora*	fairly common
	Smooth Forked Nailwort	*Paronychia canadensis*	occasional
e	Forked Chickweed	*Paronychia fastigiata*	rare
a	Bouncing Bet	*Saponaria officinalis*	common
a	White Campion / Evening Lychnis	*Silene (Lychnis) alba*	abundant
	Sleepy Catchfly	*Silene antirrhina*	rare
a	Sweet-William Catchfly	*Silene armeria*	rare
a	Wild Pink	*Silene caroliniana v. pensylvanica*	occasional
a	Night-flowering Catchfly	*Silene noctiflora*	uncommon
	Starry Campion	*Silene stellata*	uncommon
a	Bladder Campion	*Silene vulgaris (cucubalus)*	common
a	Corn Spurrey	*Spergula arvensis*	rare
a	Saltmarsh Sand-Spurrey	*Spergularia marina*	very rare
	Star Chickweed	*Stellaria corei*	occasional
a	Lesser Stitchwort	*Stellaria graminea*	fairly common
	Long-leaved Chickweed	*Stellaria longifolia*	uncommon
a	Common Chickweed	*Stellaria media*	fairly common
	Star Chickweed	*Stellaria pubera*	uncommon

BUCKWHEAT FAMILY – Polygonaceae [21]

a	Common Buckwheat	*Fagopyrum sagittatum (esculentum)*	rare
a	India-Wheat	*Fagopyrum tataricum*	escape
	Halberd-leaved Tearthumb	*Polygonum arifolium*	rare
a	Prostrate Knotweed	*Polygonum aviculare*	fairly common
	Fringed Bindweed	*Polygonum cilinode*	rare
a	Black Bindweed	*Polygonum convolvulus*	uncommon
a	Japanese Knotweed	*Polygonum cuspidatum*	uncommon
	Erect Knotweed	*Polygonum erectum*	rare
a	Common Smartweed	*Polygonum hydropiper*	common
a	Prince's-Feather	*Polygonum orientale*	escape
	Pennsylvania Smartweed	*Polygonum pensylvanicum*	common
a	Lady's-Thumb	*Polygonum persicaria*	common
	Water Smartweed	*Polygonum punctatum*	fairly common
	Arrow-leaved Tearthumb	*Polygonum sagittatum*	common
	Climbing False Buckwheat	*Polygonum scandens*	common
	Virginia Knotweed	*Polygonum virginianum (Tovara virginiana)*	fairly common
a	Sheep Sorrel	*Rumex acetosella*	abundant
a	Curled Dock	*Rumex crispus*	abundant
a	Bitter Dock	*Rumex obtusifolius*	fairly common
	Water Dock	*Rumex orbiculatus*	very rare
	Swamp Dock	*Rumex verticillatus*	very rare

ST. JOHNSWORT FAMILY – Clusiaceae [11]

	Canadian St. Johnswort	*Hypericum canadense*	occasional
e	Bushy St. Johnswort	*Hypericum densiflorum*	very rare
	Disguised St. Johnswort	*Hypericum dissimulatum*	very rare
	Pale St. Johnswort	*Hypericum ellipticum*	fairly common
	Pineweed	*Hypericum gentianoides*	uncommon
	Dwarf St. Johnswort	*Hypericum mutilum*	common
a	Common St. Johnswort	*Hypericum perforatum*	abundant
	Shrubby St. Johnswort	*Hypericum prolificum (spathulatum)*	fairly common
	Spotted St. Johnswort	*Hypericum punctatum*	common

ST. JOHNSWORT FAMILY – continued   **Status**

___	**Marsh St. Johnswort**	*Triadenum fraseri (Hypericum virginicum in part)* uncommon
___	**Marsh St. Johnswort**	*Triadenum virginicum (Hypericum virginicum in part)* uncommon

MALLOW FAMILY – Malvaceae [6]

___ *a*	**Velvet-Leaf**	*Abutilon theophrasti*	uncommon
___ *a*	**Marsh Mallow**	*Althaea officinalis*	rare
___ *a*	**Flower-of-an-Hour**	*Hibiscus trionum*	occasional
___ *a*	**Musk Mallow**	*Malva moschata*	abundant
___ *a*	**Cheeses / Common Mallow**	*Malva neglecta*	common
___ *a*	**High Mallow**	*Malva sylvestris*	rare

PITCHER-PLANT FAMILY – Sarraceniaceae [1]

___	**Pitcher-Plant**	*Sarracenia purpurea*	rare

SUNDEW FAMILY – Droseraceae [1]

___	**Round-leaved Sundew**	*Drosera rotundifolia*	rare

ROCKROSE FAMILY – Cistaceae [2]

___	**Pinweed**	*Lechea intermedia*	rare
___	**Pinweed**	*Lechea pulchella*	rare

VIOLET FAMILY – Violaceae [27]   P=Purple{13}, W=White{8}, Y=Yellow{5}

___	**Green Violet**	*Hybanthus concolor*	**Green!**	rare
___	**Hooked-spur Violet**	*Viola adunca*	**P**	rare
___	**Le Conte's Violet**	*Viola affinis*	**P**	rare
___ *a*	**European Field Pansy**	*Viola arvensis*	**Y**	rare
___	**Sweet White Violet**	*Viola blanda*	**W**	common
___	**Canada Violet**	*Viola canadensis*	**W**	fairly common
___	**Dog Violet**	*Viola conspersa*	**P**	common
___	**Marsh Blue Violet**	*Viola cucullata*	**P**	common
___	**Smooth Yellow Violet**	*Viola eriocarpa (pensylvanica)*	**Y**	fairly common
___	**Northern Downy Violet**	*Viola fimbriatula*	**P**	common
___	**Halberd-leaved Violet**	*Viola hastata*	**Y**	fairly common
___	**Southern Wood Violet**	*Viola hirsutula*	**P**	occasional
___	**Large-leaved Violet**	*Viola incognita*	**W**	very rare
___	**Lance-leaved Violet**	*Viola lanceolata*	**W**	rare
___	**Broad-leaved Wood Violet**	*Viola latiuscula*	**P**	occasional
___	**Northern White Violet**	*Viola macloskeyi (pallens)*	**W**	fairly common
___	**Early Blue (or Wood) Violet**	*Viola palmata (triloba, in part)*	**P**	uncommon
___	**Primrose-leaved Violet**	*Viola primulifolia*	**W**	occasional
___	**Downy Yellow Violet**	*Viola pubescens*	**Y**	fairly common
___	**Field Pansy / Johnny-Jump-Up**	*Viola rafinesquii (kitaibeliana)*	**W**	fairly common
___	**Long-spurred Violet**	*Viola rostrata*	**P**	fairly common
___	**Round-leaved Yellow Violet**	*Viola rotundifolia*	**Y**	fairly common
___	**Arrow-leaved Violet**	*Viola sagittata*	**P**	uncommon
___	**Great-spurred Violet**	*Viola selkirkii*	**P**	rare
___	**Common (or Woolly) Blue Violet**	*Viola sororia (papilionacea)*	**P**	common
___	**Cream (or Pale or Striped) Violet**	*Viola striata*	**W**	uncommon
___ *e*	**Appalachian Violet**	*Viola walteri (appalachiensis)*	**P**	occasional

GOURD FAMILY – Cucurbitaceae [2]

___	**Wild Cucumber / Balsam-Apple**	*Echinocystis lobata*	occasional
___	**Bur-Cucumber**	*Sicyos angulatus*	occasional

CRESS / MUSTARD FAMILY – Brassicaceae (Cruciferae) [35]   **Status**

___	a	Garlic Mustard	*Alliaria petiolata (officinalis)*	abundant
___		Sicklepod	*Arabis canadensis*	fairly common
___		Tower Mustard	*Arabis glabra*	very rare
___	e	Hairy Rock Cress	*Arabis hirsuta*	very rare
___		Smooth Rock Cress	*Arabis laevigata*	fairly common
___		Lyre-leaved Rock Cress	*Arabis lyrata*	occasional
___	a	Early Winter Cress	*Barbarea verna*	rare
___	a	Winter Cress	*Barbarea vulgaris*	abundant
___	a	Brown Mustard	*Brassica juncea*	occasional
___	a	Black Mustard	*Brassica nigra*	occasional
___	a	Field Mustard / Rape	*Brassica rapa*	occasional
___	a	Littlepod False Flax	*Camelina microcarpa*	rare
___	a	Common False Flax	*Camelina sativa*	rare
___	a	Shepherd's Purse	*Capsella bursa-pastoris*	common
___		Slender Toothwort	*Cardamine angustata (Dentaria heterophylla)*	uncommon
___		Spring Cress	*Cardamine bulbosa*	fairly common
___		Cut-leaved Toothwort	*Cardamine concatenata (Dentaria laciniata)*	common
___		Toothwort / Pepperwort	*Cardamine (Dentaria) diphylla*	fairly common
___	a	Hairy Bittercress	*Cardamine hirsuta*	rare
___	a	Small-flowered Bittercress	*Cardamine parviflora*	rare
___		Pennsylvania Bittercress	*Cardamine pensylvanica*	common
___		Mountain Watercress	*Cardamine rotundifolia*	fairly common
___	a	Vernal Whitlow-Grass	*Erophila (Draba) verna*	occasional
___	a	Treacle (or Wormseed) Mustard	*Erysimum cheiranthoides*	rare
___	a	Dame's Rocket	*Hesperis matronalis*	abundant
___	a	Cow-Cress / Field Peppergrass	*Lepidium campestre*	common
___	a	Poor-Man's-Pepper	*Lepidium virginicum*	fairly common
___	a	Watercress	*Nasturtium officinale*	fairly common
___	a	Wild Radish	*Raphanus raphanistrum*	occasional
___	a	Radish	*Raphanus sativus*	escape
___		Yellow Cress	*Rorippa palustris*	fairly common
___	a	Creeping Yellow Cress	*Rorippa sylvestris*	rare
___	a	Charlock	*Sinapis arvensis (Brassica kaber)*	fairly common
___	a	Tumble Mustard	*Sisymbrium altissimum*	uncommon
___	a	Hedge Mustard	*Sisymbrium officinale*	uncommon

HEATH FAMILY – Ericaceae [2]   see more Ericaceae in *Trees & Shrubs*

___	Trailing Arbutus	*Epigaea repens*	uncommon
___	Wintergreen / Teaberry	*Gaultheria procumbens*	fairly common

WINTERGREEN FAMILY – Pyrolaceae [4]

___	Spotted Wintergreen	*Chimaphila maculata*	occasional
___	Pipsissewa	*Chimaphila umbellata*	occasional
___	Round-leaved Pyrola	*Pyrola americana (rotundifolia)*	fairly common
___	Shinleaf	*Pyrola elliptica*	occasional

INDIAN-PIPE FAMILY – Monotropaceae [2]

___	Pinesap	*Monotropa hypopithys*	uncommon
___	Indian-Pipe	*Monotropa uniflora*	fairly common

PRIMROSE FAMILY – Primulaceae [6]

___	Fringed Loosestrife	*Lysimachia ciliata*	fairly common
___	Lance-leaved Loosestrife	*Lysimachia lanceolata*	rare

TREES & SHRUBS of Somerset County, PA

General:

Knowing the trees is arguably the litmus test for a true woodsman. The knowledge is integral to the activities of sportsmen and naturalists alike. Many sorts of people take pride in knowing which trees are which and what their uses are. Woodworkers can identify the origin (often to species) of their wood just by looking at the grain pattern, and maple syrup producers easily recognize **sugar maples** without benefit of leaves in late winter. Mushroom hunters learn tree types to increase their chances of finding certain species, and many children learn the generic outlines of **maple** and **oak** leaves. Certainly, most among us revel in the beauty of prime fall foliage whether we know the trees or not.

Trees are useful to people in many ways: lumber, fruits, furniture, heat, windbreaks, Christmas trees, kids' tree houses, lawn ornamentation, shade, and even breathing – as trees produce a lot of oxygen via the process of photosynthesis. To wildlife, trees mean food, shelter, and security. Standing dead trees may hold little value to man, but are invaluable to forest dwellers that continue to use them as homes and food sources for many years, continuing after they've fallen.

Identifying trees can be accomplished using various physical features of the tree: leaf or needle shape and arrangement, bark, buds, flowers, cones, seeds, and general form. As for all of life, "major on the majors, minor on the minors" is good advice for beginning to learn the trees, so learn the common ones first. Focus on leaves and their particulars initially – that is the most widely employed method of identification and is the usual starting point for beginners. You will notice when you are with experienced woodsmen that they will look first at the shape of the tree and the character of its bark: leaves are studied only to confirm what they already suspect, or in the event the tree is unfamiliar. As you are learning these details, you will eventually notice this transition in your own approach to identities. After you've found a new one, read about it in field guides or tree books. And be prepared for considerable differences in appearance from young to old individuals as well as crowded (dense woodland) vs. open (field) conditions. While consulting guides, remember that different books occasionally employ different common names. *Ilex montana* is called **mountain winterberry** in the *Audubon Society Guide* and **largeleaf holly** in the *Peterson Guide*: this demonstrates the importance of Latin nomenclature.

To many folks (sometimes myself included), any distant grove of evergreens is, by default, referred to as **pine** trees. But we have lots of **hemlock, spruce,** and **larch,** in the county as well, plus some planted **firs.** These are all cone bearers, or "conifers", and together they form a class of plants called *Gymnospermae*. This class of plants bears seeds not enclosed in an ovary. *Angiospermae* is the other major class and includes all flowering plants (with seeds *in* ovaries). Most of our trees are angiosperms.

As with much of the land east of the Mississippi, Somerset County woodlands formerly included large amounts of **American chestnut** *(Castanea dentata)*. Over two *billion* trees existed east of the Mississippi River in the late 19th century before the blight hit, and one of every four hardwood trees in this county was a **chestnut.** This tree was the pre-eminent hardwood over all others, and was used extensively in rural economies. The trees' annual nut harvest fed livestock and people, as well as wildlife like deer, bear and turkey. And the timber was prized for numerous uses. When the fungal blight first hit in 1904, it spread rapidly, and by 1950 most **chestnut** trees were simply gone. We still have some sizable examples left in our woodlands, but they virtually all succumb to the blight after they reach canopy height. Shoots may still be found as well, coming off the remaining stumps of trees felled by the blight. However, there is a positive side to this saga – we will soon have disease-resistant strains of **American chestnut** thanks to tremendous amounts of work done by researchers. They'll be planted in earnest starting around the year 2006 and the **chestnut** may again return to its sovereign position in the wilds around us.

Where & When:

Avoid trying to learn about trees in public parks and urban lawns where many ornamentals and exotics have been planted – they may cause quick discouragement, as most aren't included in field guides. There are a number of introduced trees, common in our region, which did not grow here as natives. For example: **blue spruce** is found all over Somerset County, but is native to the western United States. The beautiful **weeping willow** is native to China. **Blue spruce** and **weeping willow** present here now were all planted. They do not yet reproduce here naturally.

Driving backcountry roads with low traffic affords frequent stops and can yield many new and interesting species to learn – try it in all seasons. Finding mature stands of trees is difficult though, as the value of timber often seals a stands' fate before that stage. Many trees are particular to a habitat type, so check everywhere from river bottoms **(sycamore)** to mountain-tops **(mountain-ash)** for good variety.

TREES & SHRUBS of Somerset County, PA

Facts & Figures:

➤ *Trees* have a single trunk or stem whereas *shrubs/bushes* have a stem that divides into many stems at or near the ground. *Trees* are mostly 15 feet or more tall at maturity, *bushes* mostly less than that.

➤ Woodlands cover over 60% of the total land area in the county. Farmers own roughly 40%, private concerns hold 45%, forest industries claim 2%, and the state owns about 12 % of the woodlands.

➤ **Maple** syrup is a North American original and American Indians are credited with it's discovery.

➤ **Sugar** and **black maples** are best for syrup production, but any of the other maples may be tapped.

➤ It takes about 40 gallons of **maple** sugar water to produce 1 gallon of syrup. There are roughly 4000 drops per gallon, and about 20,000 gallons of syrup are produced in this county annually (we rank high in production for the state), so *3.2 billion* drops of sap are harvested in a given year here at home!

➤ Broad-leaved trees (those with literally broad leaves, as opposed to needle-leaved) have a lot of surface area through which large amounts of moisture are given off. Leaves are shed in the fall to avoid water loss when the roots cannot access as much soil water in the frozen ground of winter.

➤ Green *chlorophyll* pigment dominates in leaves through most of the summer. When decreasing daylight and low temperatures create an "abscission zone" in the leaf stem, no more chlorophyll is made, so other pigments already present begin to assert themselves. *Carotenoids* produce the yellows and oranges; *anthocyanins* formed from sugars produce reds and scarlets. Leaf color is also dependent on leaf minerals, leaf sugars, amount of sunlight, and weather conditions prior to changing. Warm sunny days followed by cool nights intensify the brilliant reds we see in autumn. Some falls are more spectacular than others, but "marvelous" is as bad as it gets here in the Laurel Highlands.

➤ Animals, insects, worms, fungi, and bacteria decompose leaves that fall. In this manner, nutrient and mineral cycling are accomplished. What the tree originally took up from the soil is returned to the soil. Cycles in nature provide fascinating study.

➤ **Red maple** leaves are toxic to horses – plant something else around the paddock. **Yew** kills cattle quickly once ingested, so avoid placing this ornamental around cattle barns.

➤ Breakdown of county woodlands (according to ASCS):

Oak, Hickory	52%	Aspen, Birch	6%	White Pine	2%
Maple, Beech, Birch	24%	Chestnut Oak	6%		
Elm, Ash, Red Maple	8%	Virginia Pine, Pitch Pine	2%		

➤ For needle trees, remember: "**s**quare **s**pruce, **f**lat **f**ir, **t**amarack **t**ufts" regarding the needle shapes.

➤ Watch shrubby winter roadsides for **common winterberry holly** (*Ilex verticillata*) that may be found there, its branches festooned with many small red berries in early winter.

Some Terms of Interest:

Hard Woods	wood of broad-leaved trees (e.g., **maple**); mostly hard, but some sorts are relatively soft
Soft Woods	wood of conifers; usually softer, but a few species are very hard
Bud	undeveloped shoot, leaf, or flower protruding from a branch or stem; may be scaled
Bundle Scars	vascular pattern in *leaf scar* (where leaf was attached) that is characteristic of a given tree
Crown	the mass of branches, stems, leaves, and flowers forming the shape of the top of a tree
Dendrology	the science or study of trees; a *dendrologist* studies trees and shrubs
Gall	blister-like swelling of plant tissue caused by either a fungus or insect parasite
Grain	on cut wood; the pattern and direction, or arrangement, of fibrous tissue
Gymnosperms	class of plants (Gymnospermae); includes conifers – bearing seeds not enclosed in ovary
Lignin	substance that, with cellulose, forms the woody cell walls in woody plants
Mast	the nut production found on a forest floor (acorns, beechnuts, et al): a "mast crop"
Sugarbush	the sum group of **maple** trees from which a syrup producer harvests sap, or sugar water
Keeler/Spile	bucket placed to catch **maple** sap / the tap driven into the tree to collect the sugar water
Ornamentals	trees, some native but mostly non-native, planted for decoration near homes or in parks
Photosynthesis	the process by which plants use sunlight to produce energy (carbohydrates) and oxygen
Chlorophyll	the agent of photosynthesis; green pigment that "does the work" of that process
Pith	the spongy and innermost tissue in a stem or twig
Phloem	water moving in cells of the phloem carries sugars from the leaves <u>down</u> to the roots;
(as "<u>flow</u>-em")	phloem and xylem are a tree's circulatory system; phloem is peripheral, xylem is central
Xylem	the inverse of phloem's path, the vascular channels for water to travel <u>up</u> the tree.
Wormy Chestnut	**American chestnut** wood that bears the scars of insect migration.

TREES & SHRUBS of Somerset County, PA

Activities:

- On the chapter list, check all of the trees/shrubs that you have found. Make notes on where and when.
- Visit a **maple sugar camp** in late February or March – the smells and tastes are delicious! And volunteers are often welcome to help gather the sugar water or fuel the fire.
- Anyone can make small amounts of syrup in their own kitchen. Contact Penn State Ag Extension (see **Appendix**) in Somerset for more information.
- As you identify a tree near your home, label it and check it in the winter to learn it without foliage.
- **Red-headed Woodpeckers** like open **oak** stands, **Yellow-throated Warblers** like **sycamore** trees, **morel** mushrooms like **ash** trees, and the pretty wildflower **beechdrops** requires **beech** trees. Many insect species depend on one or two plant species for survival. Try to learn associations such as these to broaden your enjoyment of the natural world.
- Compare your "big trees" to those listed here: www.dcnr.state.pa.us/stateparks/natural/bigtree.htm#laurel.
- Make a leaf collection: press between paper towels in a book for 10 days to dry; seal them in lamination. Another leaf collection option: rake a giant pile and tunnel with the kids into and under it.
- Drive about the county during leaf season. The colors in our county are spectacular – and second to none. The Chamber of Commerce (see **Appendix**) distributes pamphlets with suggested routes included.
- Take note of which trees near your house turn which colors in the fall and compare from year to year.
- Ponder the following wood products and try to learn why some woods are better than others for such uses: **hickory** rockers, **pine** scent, **maple** syrup, wormy **chestnut** furniture, **oak** cabinets, **cedar** chests, **sassafras** tea, **locust** fence posts, and **ash** baseball bats.
- Teach a child to count the rings on a cut stump in order to tell the age in years. Light colored wood rings are *spring wood* and the dark colored rings are *summer wood* – the pair together equals a year's growth. All the rings represent xylem; the "heartwood" is the darker part at the center of the stump.
- Check out the Pennsylvania Bureau of Forestry website: www.dcnr.state.pa.us/forestry/forestry.htm.
- Also visit The Pennsylvania Forestry Association's pages: www.cas.psu.edu/docs/casdept/forest/pfa.html.

County Status Codes:

Some of the alien trees have not been documented to reproduce here on their own yet. Nonetheless, they are familiar trees and so are listed. More such trees could probably be included. A few of the trees shown as being uncommon (county-wide) below will actually be common and easy to find in appropriate habitats. Conversely, a *common* tree may be absent in certain areas.

Abundant	occurs as a predominant tree or shrub in the county
Common	easily found, maybe in large numbers at some places
Fairly Common	not as numerous, but still able to find relatively easily
Uncommon	more scattered occurrence; may take a little effort to locate – check the right habitat
Occasional	harder to find; plan on a long look – but it should eventually be rewarded
Rare	very few in number and/or locations: good luck!
Extirpated?	it is presumed that the plant no longer occurs in Somerset County
Escape	escaped-from-cultivation, or similar situation; implies scarce and not well naturalized

a	aliens that are escaped from cultivation, or introduced and established (15)
e	endangered or threatened species (or potentially so) in Pennsylvania (9)
p	planted aliens not reproducing – but common as ornamentals and likely to be encountered (11) [Some native species are occasionally planted as ornamentals, e.g., **redbud** and **sycamore**. **Sycamore** is sometimes encountered as the hybrid **London planetree**.]

Scientific nomenclature follows Rhoads and Block (see **Sources**). Alternate scientific names for selected species are found in parentheses. Preference was usually given to the common names encountered in *Peterson's Field Guide* (Petrides)*;* selected alternate common names appear as well. As with all classes of organisms, there exists disagreement among taxonomists over nomenclature of various species of trees and most guides do not reference alternative scientific names. For those interested, consult the USDA web site plants.usda.gov for alternate nomenclature. Forty-one families are listed – some appear in the *Wildflowers* chapter as well.

TREES & SHRUBS of Somerset County, PA

Species: [185] Additions are likely, but relatively few.

Class Gymnospermae

		PINE FAMILY – Pinaceae [12]		**Status**
____	*p*	**European Larch** (most local larch are ***a/p***)	*Larix decidua*	fairly common
____	*p*	**Japanese Larch**	*Larix kaempferi*	uncommon
____		**Tamarack / American Larch**	*Larix laricina*	rare
____	*p*	**Norway Spruce**	*Picea abies*	common
____		**Black Spruce**	*Picea mariana*	rare
____	*p*	**Blue Spruce**	*Picea pungens*	fairly common
____		**Red (or Norway) Pine**	*Pinus resinosa*	occasional
____		**Pitch Pine**	*Pinus rigida*	uncommon
____		**Eastern White Pine**	*Pinus strobus*	fairly common
____	*a*	**Scotch Pine**	*Pinus sylvestris*	fairly common
____		**Virginia Pine**	*Pinus virginiana*	occasional
____		**Eastern Hemlock** *STATE TREE!*	*Tsuga canadensis*	common

		JUNIPER FAMILY – Cupressaceae [3]		
____	*p*	**Northern White-Cedar / Arbor-Vitae**	*Thuja occidentalis*	uncommon
____	*p*	**Common Juniper**	*Juniperus communis*	uncommon
____		**Eastern Redcedar**	*Juniperus virginiana*	occasional

		YEW FAMILY – Taxaceae [1]		
____	*e*	**American Yew**	*Taxus canadensis*	occasional

Class Angiospermae (all Dicot subclass)

		MAGNOLIA FAMILY – Magnoliaceae [2]		
____		**Tulip-Tree / Yellow Poplar**	*Liriodendron tulipifera*	common
____		**Cucumber Magnolia**	*Magnolia acuminata*	fairly common

		CUSTARD-APPLE FAMILY – Annonaceae [1]		
____		**Tall Pawpaw**	*Asimina triloba*	uncommon

		LAUREL FAMILY – Lauraceae [2]		
____		**Common Spicebush**	*Lindera benzoin*	common
____		**Sassafras**	*Sassafras albidum*	common

		PLANE-TREE FAMILY – Platanaceae [1]		
____		**Sycamore**	*Platanus occidentalis*	uncommon

		WITCH-HAZEL FAMILY – Hamamelidaceae [1]		
____		**Common Witch-Hazel**	*Hamamelis virginiana*	common

		ELM FAMILY – Ulmaceae [2]		
____		**American Elm**	*Ulmus americana*	rare
____		**Slippery Elm**	*Ulmus rubra*	fairly common

		MULBERRY FAMILY – Moraceae [2]		
____	*a*	**White Mulberry**	*Morus alba*	rare
____		**Red Mulberry**	*Morus rubra*	rare

TREES & SHRUBS of Somerset County, PA

WALNUT FAMILY – Juglandaceae [5]

			Status
____	**Bitternut Hickory**	*Carya cordiformis*	uncommon
____	**Pignut Hickory**	*Carya glabra*	fairly common
____	**Shagbark Hickory**	*Carya ovata*	abundant
____	**Butternut**	*Juglans cinerea*	fairly common
____	**Black Walnut**	*Juglans nigra*	fairly common

BAYBERRY FAMILY – Myricaceae [1]

____	**Sweet-fern**	*Comptonia peregrina*	uncommon

BEECH FAMILY – Fagaceae [12]

____	**American Chestnut**	*Castanea dentata*	uncommon
____	**Beech**	*Fagus grandifolia*	fairly common
____	**White Oak**	*Quercus alba*	abundant
____	**Scarlet Oak**	*Quercus coccinea*	fairly common
____	**Scrub** (or **Bear**) **Oak**	*Quercus ilicifolia*	occasional
____	**Shingle Oak**	*Quercus imbricaria*	occasional
____	**Chestnut Oak**	*Quercus montana (prinus)*	common
____	**Chinquapin Oak**	*Quercus muhlenbergii*	rare
____	**Pin Oak**	*Quercus palustris*	occasional
____	**Dwarf** (or **Chinquapin**) **Oak**	*Quercus prinoides*	rare
____	**Red Oak**	*Quercus rubra*	abundant
____	**Black Oak**	*Quercus velutina*	uncommon

BIRCH FAMILY – Betulaceae [9]

____	**Speckled Alder**	*Alnus incana (rugosa)*	fairly common
____	**Smooth Alder**	*Alnus serrulata*	uncommon
____	**Yellow Birch**	*Betula alleghaniensis (lutea)*	fairly common
____	**Black** (or **Sweet**) **Birch**	*Betula lenta*	common
____ *p*	**European White Birch**	*Betula pendula*	fairly common
____	**Ironwood / Blue Beech / Hornbeam**	*Carpinus caroliniana*	common
____	**American Hazelnut / Filbert**	*Corylus americana*	fairly common
____	**Beaked Hazelnut**	*Corylus cornuta*	rare
____	**Hophornbeam**	*Ostrya virginiana*	common

LINDEN FAMILY – Tiliaceae [1]

____	**American Basswood**	*Tilia americana* var. *americana*	fairly common
	White Basswood____	*Tilia americana* var. *heterophylla*	uncommon

WILLOW FAMILY – Salicaceae [13]

____	**Eastern Cottonwood**	*Populus deltoides*	occasional
____	**Bigtooth Aspen**	*Populus grandidentata*	fairly common
____	**Quaking Aspen**	*Populus tremuloides*	uncommon
____ *a*	**White Willow**	*Salix alba*	occasional
____ *p*	**Weeping Willow**	*Salix babylonica*	fairly common
____	**Long-beaked** (or **Gray**) **Willow**	*Salix bebbiana*	rare
____	**Pussy Willow**	*Salix discolor*	uncommon
____	**Heart-leaved Willow**	*Salix eriocephala (rigida)*	fairly common
____	**Tall Prairie Willow**	*Salix humilis*	uncommon
____	**Shining Willow**	*Salix lucida*	rare
____	**Black Willow**	*Salix nigra*	common
____ *e*	**Meadow Willow**	*Salix petiolaris (gracilis)*	rare
____	**Silky Willow**	*Salix sericea*	common

TREES & SHRUBS of Somerset County, PA

HEATH FAMILY – Ericaceae [19]   see more Ericaceae in *Wildflowers*   **Status**

____	Leatherleaf	*Chamaedaphne calyculata*	rare
____	Black Huckleberry	*Gaylussacia baccata*	fairly common
____	Mountain Laurel **STATE FLOWER!**	*Kalmia latifolia*	common
____	Maleberry	*Lyonia ligustrina*	uncommon
____ e	Minniebush	*Menziesia pilosa*	rare
____	Sourwood	*Oxydendrum arboreum*	rare
____	Smooth Azalea	*Rhododendron arborescens*	fairly common
____ e	Flame Azalea	*Rhododendron calendulaceum*	PA extirpated?
____	Great Rhododendron	*Rhododendron maximum*	common
____	Pink Azalea	*Rhododendron periclymenoides (nudiflorum)*	fairly common
____	Early (or Mountain) Azalea	*Rhododendron prinophyllum (roseum)*	fairly common
____	Swamp-Pink / Swamp Azalea	*Rhododendron viscosum*	uncommon
____	Late Low Blueberry	*Vaccinium angustifolium*	common
____	Common Highbush Blueberry	*Vaccinium corymbosum*	rare
____	Large Cranberry	*Vaccinium macrocarpon*	uncommon
____	Velvetleaf Blueberry	*Vaccinium myrtilloides*	rare
____	Small Cranberry	*Vaccinium oxycoccos*	occasional
____	Early Low Blueberry	*Vaccinium pallidum (vacillans)*	common
____	Tall Deerberry	*Vaccinium stamineum*	uncommon

HYDRANGEA FAMILY – Hydrangeaceae [1]

____	Seven-Bark / Wild Hydrangea	*Hydrangea arborescens*	uncommon

GOOSEBERRY FAMILY – Grossulariaceae [5]

____	Wild Black Currant	*Ribes americanum*	occasional
____	Prickly Gooseberry	*Ribes cynosbati*	fairly common
____	Currant / Gooseberry	*Ribes glandulosum*	rare
____	Swamp Black Currant	*Ribes lacustre*	rare
____	Round-leaved Gooseberry	*Ribes rotundifolium*	fairly common

ROSE FAMILY – Rosaceae [23]   see more Rosaceae in *Wildflowers*

____	Downy Juneberry / Sarvis / Serviceberry	*Amelanchier arborea*	common
____ e	Low Juneberry	*Amelanchier humilis*	rare
____	Swamp Juneberry	*Amelanchier intermedia*	uncommon
____	Smooth Juneberry	*Amelanchier laevis*	uncommon
____	Running Juneberry	*Amelanchier stolonifera*	occasional
____	Red Chokeberry	*Aronia (Pyrus) arbutifolia*	occasional
____	Black Chokeberry	*Aronia (Pyrus) melanocarpa*	fairly common
____	Purple Chokeberry	*Aronia prunifolia (Pyrus floribunda)*	fairly common
____	Pear Hawthorn	*Crataegus calopendron*	rare
____	Cockspur Hawthorn	*Crataegus crus-galli*	common
____	Scarlet Hawthorn	*Crataegus coccinea (pedicellata)*	fairly common
____	Dotted Hawthorn	*Crataegus punctata*	fairly common
____	Sweet Crabapple	*Malus (Pyrus) coronaria*	fairly common
____ a	Domestic Apple	*Malus pumila (domestica)*	escape
____	Lance-leaf Crabapple	*Malus lancifolia*	occasional
____	Ninebark	*Physocarpus opulifolius*	fairly common
____	American Plum	*Prunus americana*	uncommon
____ a	Sweet Cherry	*Prunus avium*	rare
____	Fire (or Pin) Cherry	*Prunus pensylvanica*	fairly common
____	Black Cherry	*Prunus serotina*	abundant
____	Choke Cherry	*Prunus virginiana*	common
____	American Mountain-Ash	*Sorbus (Pyrus) americana*	fairly common
____ a	Domestic Pear	*Pyrus communis*	escape

ARACHNIDS of Somerset County, PA

Species: [118] Additions are likely – more than triple the number of spider species on this list are present. However, most routinely encountered species are included below. [But many that should be reasonably common have not yet been documented locally – go get 'em!] The "spp." designation after a genus indicates the possibility of either multiple or undetermined species.

<u>Order Aranae</u> – Spiders [98]

FUNNEL WEB WEAVERS – Family Agelenidae [3]

			Status
____	**Grass Spider**	*Agelenopsis naevia*	common
____	**Funnel Weaver**	*Agelenopsis pennsylvanica*	common
____*a*	**Barn Funnel Weaver**	*Tegenaria domestica*	fairly common

HACKLEDMESH WEAVERS – Family Amaurobiidae [3]

____	no common name	*Amaurobius ferox*	fairly common
____	no common name	*Callobius bennetti*	fairly common
____	no common name	*Wadotes hybridus*	fairly common

FOLDINGDOOR SPIDERS – Family Antrodiaetidae [1]

____	no common name	*Antrodiaetus robustus*	uncommon

GHOST SPIDERS – Family Anyphaenidae [2]

____	no common name	*Anyphaena celer*	uncommon
____	no common name	*Wulfila saltabunda*	uncommon

ORB WEAVERS – Family Araneidae [24]

____	**Star-bellied Orbweaver**	*Acanthepeira stellata*	common
____	**Barn Spider**	*Araneus cavaticus*	fairly common
____*a*	**Garden Spider / "Cross Spider"**	*Araneus diadematus*	fairly common
____	**Marbled Orb Weaver**	*Araneus marmoreus*	fairly common
____	no common name	*Araneus nordmanni*	uncommon
____	no common name	*Araneus pratensis*	uncommon
____	**Lattice Orbweaver**	*Araneus thaddeus*	fairly common
____	**Shamrock Spider**	*Araneus trifolium*	common
____	**Six-spotted Orb Weaver**	*Araniella displicata*	uncommon
____	**Black-and-Yellow Argiope**	*Argiope aurantia*	common
____	**Banded Argiope** (or **B. Garden Spider**)	*Argiope trifasciata*	common
____	**Humpbacked Orbweaver**	*Eustala anastera*	fairly common
____	**Trash-line Orbweaver**	*Cyclosa conica*	uncommon
____	no common name	*Gea heptagon*	fairly common
____	no common name	*Larinia spp.*	uncommon
____	**Furrow Spider**	*Larinioides cornutus (Nuctenea cornuta)*	common
____	**Bridge Orbweaver**	*Larinioides sclopetarius*	uncommon
____	**Lined Orbweaver**	*Mangora gibberosa*	uncommon
____	**Labyrinth Orbweaver**	*Metepeira labyrinthiea*	uncommon
____	**Spined Micrathena**	*Micrathena gracilis*	uncommon
____	**White Micrathena**	*Micrathena mitrata*	uncommon
____	**Arrow-shaped Micrathena**	*Micrathena saggittata*	rare
____	**Arabesque Orbweaver**	*Neoscona arabesca*	common
____	no common name	*Neoscona pratensis*	uncommon

MESHWEB WEAVERS – Family Dictynidae [5]

____	no common name	*Dictyna foliacea*	fairly common
____	no common name	*Dictyna volucripes*	fairly common
____	no common name	*Emblyna annulipes*	fairly common
____	no common name	*Emblyna sublata*	fairly common

ARACHNIDS of Somerset County, PA

MESHWEB WEAVERS – continued **Status**

_____ no common name *Emblyna hentzi* fairly common

GROUND SPIDERS – Family Gnaphosidae [1]
_____ no common name *Zelotes spp.* uncommon

SHEET-WEB WEAVERS – Family Linyphiidae [11]

_____	no common name	*Bathyphantes pallidus*	fairly common
_____	no common name	*Diplostyla concolor*	fairly common
_____	no common name	*Drapetisca alteranda*	uncommon
_____	no common name	*Eperigone maculata*	fairly common
_____	no common name	*Erigone autumnalis*	fairly common
_____	**Bowl-and-Doily Spider**	*Frontinella pyramitela*	common
_____	no common name	*Lepthyphantes nebulosus*	uncommon
_____	**Platform Spider**	*Microlinyphia mandibulata*	fairly common
_____	**Filmy Dome Spider**	*Neriene radiata*	fairly common
_____	no common name	*Neriene variabilis*	fairly common
_____	**Hammock Spider**	*Pityohyphantes costatus*	fairly common

WOLF SPIDERS – Family Lycosidae [9]

_____	**Burrowing Wolf Spider**	*Geolycosa spp.*	uncommon
_____	**Forest Wolf Spider**	*Gladicosa (Lycosa) gulosa*	uncommon
_____	**Carolina Wolf Spider**	*Hogna (Lycosa) carolinensis*	uncommon
_____	no common name	*Hogna helluo (Lycosa nidicola)*	common
_____	**Thin-legged Wolf Spider**	*Pardosa lapidicina*	common
_____	**Thin-legged Wolf Spider**	*Pardosa saxatilis*	common
_____	**Pirate Wolf Spider**	*Pirata minutus*	fairly common
_____	**Rabid Wolf Spider**	*Rabidosa (Lycosa) rabida*	fairly common
_____	no common name	*Schizocosa avida (Lycosa communis)*	common

SAC SPIDERS – Family Miturgidae (Clubionidae) [1]
_____ *a* **Yellow Sac Spider** *Cheiracanthium mildei* uncommon

LYNX SPIDERS – Family Oxyopidae [1]
_____ **Striped Lynx Spider** *Oxyopes salticus* uncommon

PHILODROMIDS – Family Philodromidae [2]
_____ **Running Crab Spider** *Philodromus spp.* uncommon
_____ no common name *Thanatus formicinus* uncommon

DADDY-LONG-LEGS-SPIDERS – Family Pholcidae [2]
(not to be confused w/ *Phalangidae*; the harvestmen or "daddy-long-legs" on next page)
_____ **Long-bodied Cellar Spider** *Pholcus phalangioides* common
_____ **Short-bodied Cellar Spider** *Spermophora meridionalis* uncommon

NURSERY WEB SPIDERS – Family Pisauridae [3]
_____ **Six-spotted Fishing Spider** *Dolomedes triton* uncommon
_____ no common name *Dolomedes vittatus (urinator)* uncommon
_____ **Nursery Web Spider** *Pisaurina mira* fairly common

ARACHNIDS of Somerset County, PA

JUMPING SPIDERS – Family Salticidae [11]   **Status**

Bronze Jumper	*Eris militaris*	common
no common name	*Evarcha hoyi*	common
no common name	*Habrocestum pulex*	fairly common
no common name	*Habronattus spp.*	fairly common
no common name	*Hentzia palmarum*	common
Dimorphic Jumping Spider	*Maevia inclemens*	fairly common
no common name	*Metacyrba undata*	uncommon
Peppered Jumper	*Pelegrina (Metaphidippus) galathea*	fairly common
Zebra Jumper	*Salticus scenicus*	common
Bold Jumper	*Phidippus audax*	common
no common name	*Phidippus clarus*	common

LONG-JAWED ORB WEAVERS – Family Tetragnathidae [4]

Orchard Spider	*Leucauge venusta*	fairly common
Long-jawed Orbweaver	*Tetragnatha elongata*	uncommon
Silver Long-jawed Orbweaver	*Tetragnatha laboriosa*	fairly common
no common name	*Tetragnatha versicolor*	fairly common

COMB-FOOTED SPIDERS – Family Theridiidae [7]

American House Spider	*Achaearanea tepidariorum*	fairly common
Dewdrop Spider	*Argyrodes trigonum*	uncommon
Northern Black Widow Spider	*Latrodectus variolus*	rare
no common name	*Steatoda borealis*	fairly common
no common name	*Steatoda triangulosa*	fairly common
no common name	*Theridion frondeum*	fairly common
no common name	*Theridion glaucescens*	uncommon

CRAB SPIDERS – Family Thomisidae [7]

Goldenrod Spider	*Misumena vatia*	fairly common
Northern Crab Spider	*Misumenops asperatus*	common
Red-banded Crab Spider	*Misumenoides spp.*	common
no common name	*Xysticus auctificus*	uncommon
Elegant Crab Spider	*Xysticus elegans*	fairly common
no common name	*Xysticus funestus*	uncommon
Thrice-banded Crab Spider	*Xysticus triguttatus*	uncommon

TITANOECIDS – Family Titanoecidae [1]

no common name	*Titanoeca americana*	fairly common

Order Opilones – Harvestmen [2]

Eastern Daddy-long-legs	*Leiobunum spp.*	common
Brown Daddy-long-legs	*Phalangium opilio*	common

Order Acarina – Mites & Ticks [18]

MITES

Cheyletiella Mange Mite	*Cheyletiella spp.*	rare
Chorioptic Mange Mite (mostly cattle)	*Chorioptes bovis*	fairly common
Demodectic Mange (dogs)	*Demodex canis*	uncommon
Knemidocoptic Mange Mite (parakeets)	*Knemidocoptes pilae*	uncommon
Notoedric Mange Mite (cats, et al)	*Notoedres cati*	rare
Cat / Dog Ear Mites	*Otodectes cynotis*	common
Rabbit Ear Mite / Ear Canker	*Psoroptes cuniculi*	common
Sarcoptic Mange Mite (mostly dogs)	*Sarcoptes scabiei*	uncommon

ARACHNIDS of Somerset County, PA

		Status
Order Acarina – continued		**Status**
____ **Guinea Pig Mange Mite**	*Trixacarus caviae*	rare
____ **Velvet Mite**	*Trombidium spp.*	fairly common

TICKS

____ **Groundhog Tick**	*Ixodes cooki*	rare
____ **Black-legged Tick (Deer Tick)**	*Ixodes scapularis (daminii)*	uncommon
____ **Rabbit Tick**	*Ixodes dentatus*	uncommon
____ **Winter Tick**	*Dermacentor albipictus*	uncommon
____ **American Dog Tick**	*Dermacentor variabilis*	uncommon
____ **Lone Star Tick**	*Amblyoma americanum*	rare
____ soft bat tick	*Ornithodoros kelleyi*	fairly common
____ soft poultry tick	*Ornithodorus spp.*	uncommon

Reviewed by:

Richard A. Bradley, Ph.D. – Associate Professor, EEO Biology, The Ohio State University

Sources:

Emerton, James H., and S.W. Frost. 1961. *The Common Spiders of the United States.* Dover Publications, Inc., New York. 227 pp.

Georgi, Jay R. 1985. *Parasitology for Veterinarians.* W. B. Saunders Co., Philadelphia. 344 pp.

Kaston, B.J. 1981. *Spiders of Connecticut.* Conn. Department of Environmental Protection, Hartford. 1020 pp. (available at Connecticut Department of Environmental Protection for ~$25)

Levi, Herbert W. 1968. *Spiders and Their Kin (A Golden Guide).* Golden Press, New York. 160 pp.

Milne, Lorus, and Margery Milne. 1984. *The Audubon Society Field Guide to North American Insects & Spiders.* Alfred A. Knopf, New York. 989 pp.

▶ Many so-called "spider bites" are actually the handiwork of a number of different insect species. But true spider bites do occasionally occur. Around our parts, the **yellow sac spider** probably accounts for more of these bites than any other spider species. Some people react strongly to their venom and those incidents may be mistakenly blamed on **brown recluse**, which are quite rare in Pennsylvania.

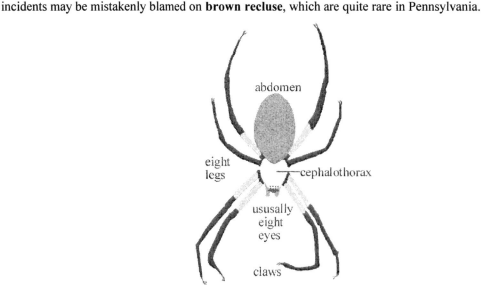

Figure 5 – Spider Topography

INSECTS of Somerset County, PA

General:

Insects are members of the phylum Arthropoda and so have the hard exoskeleton (hard outer body) characteristic of arthropods. But they are set apart from other arthropods by exhibiting three body sections: head, thorax, and abdomen. Attached to the thorax are **three pairs of legs** (vs. the *four* pairs of legs on arachnids). Many members of the class Insecta also have one or two pairs of membranous wings. Because of the large numbers involved, entomologists often devote their study to just one order within the class of insects rather than attempt competence with all of the 29 different orders.

It is somewhat ironic that the class of biota responsible for the largest diversity of species to our county will receive, relatively, the shallowest treatment. The class Insecta has the largest number of representatives in the world with over <u>one</u> <u>million</u> known species. Insects are the most numerous creatures in this county . . . or about anywhere for that matter. There are, in fact, so many "bugs" here that a comprehensive summary would be very difficult indeed. Identification to species for many insects is often based on technical or microscopic features that are typically of little interest to the layman (some listings below are taken only to a family or genus level). Additionally, there aren't many collections kept in the county; nor are there as many amateur entomologists recording observations as there are, say, birders or fishermen. Most of the species included here are ones that common field guides cover; and those guides offer (again, out of necessity) a relatively shallow treatment. If one should want to know more, manuals are available that tackle only given orders or families of insects, and so are far more comprehensive than standard field guides. Contact BioQuip (see **Appendix**) for a listing of pertinent literature.

Given this perspective, it may be understood why most of the order summaries in this chapter fall far short of what's actually out there. Some orders are well represented – the list of stoneflies may be more than most of us care to assimilate. However, a scan of all the species below shows that the average reader is already familiar with many of our insects. We learn at a young age about **flies, mosquitoes, bees, lightning bugs, beetles, butterflies, moths,** and even **praying mantises.**

Insects are often thought of as "pesky", but less than 1% of insects nationwide are considered serious pests. However, some earn that classification well because of damage to crops or structures, by disease transmission, by their annoying character **(blackflies),** or in some other way interfering with man's interests. Damages every year run in the multi-billions nationwide and farmers raising crops in Somerset County must use chemical control to keep the damage down. Happily, other insect species compensate for the sins of their brethern. If not through the myriad number of flowers they pollinate or the bigger animals they feed, then through the simple joy we have of watching **lightning bugs** blink, hearing the **katydids'** evening symphony, or chasing **dragonflies** as they skirt the pond's edge.

Butterflies and **moths,** an order of insects, have been given their own chapter. They are unusual among the *Insecta* in that many species may be separated visually by using available field guides.

Most of us who have been stung don't care much for our various bees. On the other hand, **honeybees** enjoy a sort of diplomatic immunity – we do like to eat honey! Honeybees, which are not native to North America, have undergone a precipitous decline in recent years due to two types of microscopic, parasitic mite species. **Bumblebees** are actually a group of species; take notice of the difference in sizes encountered. The miserable little vermin that live in the ground are **yellow jackets;** and they are aggressive! So are the **bald-faced hornets** (actually another kind of yellow jacket and not a true hornet) that make the basketball-sized, gray, paper nests hanging in trees or under the eaves of buildings.

The list goes on and on. The numbers of insect species, and population numbers overall (insects reproduce at tremendous rates), assures an inexhaustible hobby for anyone with a bent towards this fascinating class of life.

Where & When:

Winter may not seem very productive, but some insects are still easily found during that time in protected areas. The rest of the year is crawling with possibilities. On flowers and leaves, under stones and logs, at windows, around and in ponds: virtually *everywhere* is good habitat for insects. Windows in garages and barns are easy collection spots. Don't forget to check in the waters of streams and rivers as well as under rocks and logs wherever you find them. Bug poppers, though good for little otherwise, will sometimes yield interesting finds. As with the arachnids, sweep-netting a field or tree branches maximizes the numbers found. Time of day is also important – night collecting is the best for many species. This is especially true for moths, but other insects are also attracted to nightlights and can be baited in with light traps. See the chapter on butterflies and moths for more information on nighttime collecting.

INSECTS of Somerset County, PA

Facts & Figures:

➤ Scientists estimate the average insect population <u>per square mile</u> as equal to the world's human populace.

➤ This book covers about 2850 species overall, flora and fauna combined. But Somerset County probably hosts over **10,000** species of insects alone.

➤ There are over **30,000** species of <u>just</u> Coleoptera (beetles) in North America: Coleoptera is the largest order in the animal kingdom. Incredible!

➤ Other big numbers include: ~**100,000** insect species total for just North America (over **one million** worldwide) including more than: **550** Mayflies, **16,000** flies, **17,000** bees, ants, and wasps, and **1000** species of grasshopper. Roughly **600** (less than 1%) species are considered to be serious pests.

➤ **Dragonflies, or "snake doctors",** don't sting. The larger ones can give mild pinch bites, though.

➤ Bug Poppers don't take out many mosquitoes. **Bats** and **Purple Martins** are far better at mosquito control – entice them to live around your home if you don't like mosquitoes.

➤ Some social insects do dances to communicate locations of nectar sources to other colony members – **honeybees** most famous among them. Scientists have deciphered some of the honeybees' dance to the point where exact flower locations may be found hundreds of yards away.

➤ **Pennsylvania firefly** is the state insect: the flashes of light that we see in the air are from flying males trying to attract flightless females waiting in the grass to signal back to them.

➤ Some female fireflies mimic the flashes of other firefly species to lure males in . . . and then eat them!

➤ **June beetles** that you see on screen doors at night are males looking for "ladies." Females don't fly.

➤ **Earwigs** are so named for the nonsensical legend of them crawling into sleeping peoples' ears.

➤ Insects have some unconventional sensory applications: the antennae of insects are used to *smell*, **crickets** can *hear* with their legs, most insects can see ultraviolet light, and some can see infrared light.

➤ Insects don't produce their own body heat; they're "cold-blooded" (and their blood isn't red – it's green).

➤ A few **ants** are farmers of sorts – they keep colonies of **aphids** from which to extract sweet juices.

➤ No male specimens are known for certain species of insect that undergo *parthenogenesis* (see **Terms**).

➤ A **honeybee** can sting only once as part of its abdomen is sacrificed in the process – the bee then dies.

➤ It is best to leave insect larval stages or pupae outside for the winter – progression of their life cycles depends on freezing temperatures for many species.

Terms of Interest:

Ecdysis	molting or shedding of an insect's exoskeleton, or "skin"
Eggs	Insects are egg-layers – some species' eggs develop internally
Entomology	the science devoted to studying insects; *entomologists* are scientists who study insects
Elytron	thickened forewing covering – plural *elytra* – for the flight-giving hindwings of beetles (a **ladybug's** elytra are orange or red with black dots)
Exoskeleton	external hard supportive structure for the body; mammals have internal skeletons
Hellgrammites	**dobsonfly** larvae; often used as fishing bait for trout
Imago	adult stage of some insects e.g. **mayflies**
Insect Galls	insects lay eggs; larva hatches and <u>plant tissues swell</u> around the developing larva
Molting	the process of shedding the *exoskeleton*; also referred to as *ecdysis*
Naiad	*aquatic* young of **mayflies, stoneflies, dragonflies, damselflies;** direct change to adult
Nymph	juveniles wherein the hatched young resemble miniature adults; in <u>simple metamorphosis</u>
Instar	stage of an insect between molts – the first *instar* is between egg hatching and first molt: juveniles of either type of metamorphosis e.g., *larval instars* or *nymphal instars*
Larva	active, feeding, juvenile stage of insects that undergo <u>complete metamorphosis</u>; **beetle** larvae are *grubs*, **butterfly** and **moth** larvae are *caterpillars*, **fly** larvae are *maggots*
Proboscis	modified jaws forming a tube for feeding upon liquids such as nectar or blood
Social Insects	organized communities in which the members depend on one another (**ants, bees** et al.); most insects are *not* social
Parthenogenesis	eggs develop without fertilization
Pupa	inactive stage after last larval instar, prior to adulthood in <u>complete metamorphosis</u> (as for **beetles** and **butterflies**)
Simple Metamorphosis	juveniles *(nymphs)* resemble adults; "simple" changes to adult
Complete Metamorphosis	juveniles *(larva)* <u>do not</u> resemble adults; "complex" changes to adult
Stereo Microscope	enlarges insects three-dimensionally; helpful for complex identifications

INSECTS of Somerset County, PA

Activities:
- On the list below, check all of the insects that you have found. Make notes on where and when.
- Sweep-net a field: you'll be amazed at the sheer number of insects and spiders you'll find.
- Catch some **fireflies** and keep them in a jar for a night. **Ant farms** are interesting to keep as well.
- Start an insect collection. Valuable contributions to science are possible from this activity. Consult the various field guides for information on labeling and storing them correctly.
- Closely examine large plants and you'll find a number of dramas unfolding upon them. The biomass of insects in even a small area is astounding: on the ground, on stalks and trunks, and on the leaves.
- Examine a **bald-faced hornet's** nest in the winter. They're the classic basketball-size nests in trees.
- Take "stumper" identifications to the Ag-extension office for submission to Penn State entomologists.
- Try chasing **dragonflies** for exercise: they can fly up to 60 mph. Fortunately, we can often outrun bees.
- Listen to the nighttime cacophony of insects: learn the **katydid's** call that is very loud in late summer.
- Visit the Entomological Society of America's website at www.entsoc.org.
- Penn Sate University also maintains a nice entomology site at www.ento.psu.edu.

County Status Codes:
Many of these codes reflect the frequency with which I encountered the species as opposed to being true indicators of relative abundance. Entomologists of all levels are welcome to contribute records or status revisions.

Abundant	seen frequently and in numbers with low or no effort; can't miss
Common	usually found *readily* through the season by those who are seeking; won't miss
Fairly Common	usually able to find – but more restricted season or habitat; shouldn't miss
Uncommon	probably found *eventually* by seekers over a season – small numbers found; might miss
Occasional	sporadic and unusual – may require special habitat, probably miss
Rare	hard to find – few records; perhaps truly rare *or* easily overlooked; good luck!
a	alien species not native to the United States

Taxonomy for some orders of Insecta is currently under considerable debate. The following arrangement will serve as "good enough" for our purposes here. Scientific names were taken from a variety of sources (often following Dunn, 1996). Some alternate names are listed in parentheses. Genera are listed alphabetically.

Species: [274] Additions are likely – the overwhelming majority of species present are not listed due to complexities discussed above. This list is simply a sampling of the huge numbers of genera and species – the technical separation of many insects at the species level (and sometimes even at the family level) requires the skill of formally trained entomologists. However, most familiar insects are included below. The "spp." designation after a genus indicates the possibility of either multiple or undetermined species.

Subclass Apterygota

Order Protura – Proturans [1]

			Status
____	no common name – a probable resident	*Amerentulus americanus*	rare

Order Collembola – Springtails [1]

____	**Snow Flea**	*Hypogastrura (Achorutes) nivicola*	fairly common

Order Thysanura – Common Bristletails [2]

____	**Silverfish**	*Lepisma saccharina`*	common
____	**Firebrat**	*Thermobia domestica*	rare

INSECTS of Somerset County, PA

Subclass Pterygota
Division Exopterygota

<u>Order Ephemeroptera</u> – Mayflies [2]   <u>Status</u>

____	**Small Mayfly**	*Baetis spp.*	common
____	**Burrowing Mayfly**	*Epehemera spp.*	common

<u>Order Odonata</u> – Dragonflies & Damselflies [68]

____	**Canada Darner**	*Aeshna canadensis*	fairly common
____	**Lance-tipped Darner**	*Aeshna constricta*	fairly common
____	**Black-tipped Darner**	*Aeshna tuberculifera*	occasional
____	**Shadow Darner**	*Aeshna umbrosa*	common
____	**Green Darner**	*Anax junius*	common
____	**Comet Darner**	*Anax longipes*	occasional
____	**Blue-fronted Dancer**	*Argia apicalis*	uncommon
____	**Variable Dancer**	*Argia fumipennis*	fairly common
____	**Powdered Dancer**	*Argia moesta*	fairly common
____	**Unicorn Clubtail**	*Arigomphus villosipes*	uncommon
____	**Fawn (or Brown) Darner**	*Boyeria vinosa*	fairly common
____	**Appalachian Jewelwing**	*Calopteryx angustipennis*	occasional
____	**Black-winged Damselfly / Ebony Jewelwing**	*Calopteryx maculata*	common
____	**Calico Pennant**	*Celithemis elisa*	fairly common
____	**Banded Pennant**	*Celithemis fasciata*	uncommon
____	**Aurora Damsel**	*Chromagrion conditum*	fairly common
____	**Delta-spotted Spiketail**	*Cordulegaster diastatops*	uncommon
____	**Twin-spotted Spiketail**	*Cordulegaster maculata*	fairly common
____	**Stream Cruiser**	*Didymops transversa*	fairly common
____	**Rainbow Bluet**	*Enallagma antennatum*	fairly common
____	**Azure Bluet**	*Enallagma aspersum*	fairly common
____	**Double-striped Bluet**	*Enallagma basidens*	uncommon
____	**Familiar Bluet**	*Enallagma civile*	abundant
____	**Stream Bluet**	*Enallagma exsulans*	common
____	**Skimming Bluet**	*Enallagma geminatum*	fairly common
____	**Hagen's Bluet**	*Enallagma hageni*	fairly common
____	**Orange Bluet**	*Enallagma signatum*	fairly common
____	**Slender Bluet**	*Enallagma traviatum*	occasional
____	**Vesper Bluet**	*Enallagma vesperum*	rare
____	**Swamp Darner**	*Epiaeschna heros*	uncommon
____	**Common Baskettail**	*Epitheca (Tetragoneuria) cynosura*	fairly common
____	**Prince Baskettail**	*Epitheca princeps*	fairly common
____	**Eastern Pondhawk**	*Erythemis simplicicollis*	fairly common
____	**Mustached Clubtail**	*Gomphus adelphus*	fairly common
____	**Harpoon Clubtail**	*Gomphus descriptus*	occasional
____	**Lancet Clubtail**	*Gomphus exilis*	common
____	**Ashy Clubtail**	*Gomphus lividus*	fairly common
____	**Sable Clubtail**	*Gomphus rogersi*	rare
____	**Dragonhunter**	*Hagenius brevistylus*	fairly common
____	**Uhler's Sundragon**	*Helocordulia uhleri*	uncommon
____	**American Rubyspot**	*Hetaerina americana*	uncommon
____	**Citrine Forktail**	*Ischnura hastata*	uncommon
____	**Fragile Forktail**	*Ischnura posita*	fairly common
____	**Eastern Forktail**	*Ischnura verticalis*	common
____	**Slender Spreadwing**	*Lestes rectangularis*	fairly common
____	**Swamp Spreadwing**	*Lestes vigilax*	uncommon
____	**Dot-tailed Whiteface**	*Leucorrhinia intacta*	uncommon

OWLET MOTHS – continued

Common Name	Scientific Name	Status
Reddish Speckled Dart	*Cerastis tenebrifera*	fairly common
Snowy Dart	*Euagrotis illapsa*	fairly common
Attentive Dart	*Eueretagrotis attenta*	uncommon
Master's Dart	*Feltia herilis*	common
Dingy Cutworm Moth	*Feltia jaculifera*	abundant
Subgothic Dart	*Feltia subgothica*	fairly common
no common name	*Heptagrotis phyllophora*	fairly common
_a_ **Large Yellow Underwing**	*Noctua pronuba*	common
Flame-shouldered Dart	*Ochropleura plecta*	common
Variegated Cutworm Moth	*Peridroma saucia*	common
Clandestine Dart	*Spaelotis clandestina*	fairly common
Pale-banded Dart	*Xestia badinodis*	fairly common
Pink-spotted Dart	*Xestia bicarnea*	common
Greater Black-letter Dart	*Xestia dolosa*	common
Smith's Dart	*Xestia smithii*	common

Subfamily Hadeninae {25}

Common Name	Scientific Name	Status
Distinct Quaker	*Achatia distincta*	fairly common
no common name	*Aletia oxygala*	fairly common
The Nutmeg	*Discestra trifolii*	fairly common
Wheat Head Armyworm Moth	*Faronta diffusa*	fairly common
Scurfy Quaker	*Homorthodes furfurata*	fairly common
The Thinker	*Lacinipolia meditata*	fairly common
Olive Arches	*Lacinipolia olivacea*	uncommon
Bristly Cutworm Moth	*Lacinipolia renigera*	common
no common name	*Leucania commoides*	uncommon
Unarmed Wainscot	*Leucania inermis*	fairly common
no common name	*Leucania insueta*	uncommon
Many-lined Wainscot	*Leucania multilinea*	fairly common
Phragmites Wainscot	*Leucania phragmitidicola*	fairly common
Ursula Wainscot	*Leucania ursula*	fairly common
Confused Woodgrain	*Morrisonia confusa*	common
Fluid Arches	*Morrisonia latex*	common
Bronzed Cutworm Moth	*Nephelodes minians*	common
Rustic Quaker	*Orthodes crenulata*	fairly common
Speckled Green Fruitworm Moth	*Orthosia hibisci*	common
Ruby Quaker	*Orthosia rubescens*	uncommon
Disparaged Arches	*Polia detracta*	fairly common
Cloudy Arches	*Polia imbrifera*	fairly common
Stormy Arches	*Polia nimbosa*	fairly common
Armyworm Moth	*Pseudaletia unipuncta*	abundant
Striped Garden Caterpillar Moth	*Trichordestra legitima*	common

Subfamily Cuculliinae {22}

Common Name	Scientific Name	Status
Fringe-Tree Sallow	*Adita chionanthi*	fairly common
Dotted Sallow	*Anathix ralla*	fairly common
_a_ **Toadflax Moth**	*Calophasia lunula*	uncommon
Fawn Sallow	*Copipanolis styracis*	fairly common
Grote's Sallow	*Copivaleria grotei*	common
The Asteroid	*Cucullia asteroides*	fairly common
Brown-hooded Owlet	*Cucullia convexipennis*	uncommon
no common name	*Cucullia florea*	uncommon
Intermediate Cucullia	*Cucullia intermedia*	uncommon
Scalloped Sallow	*Eucirroedia pampina*	fairly common
Lost Sallow	*Eupsilia devia*	uncommon
Morrison's Sallow	*Eupsilia morrisoni*	abundant
Straight-toothed Sallow	*Eupsilia vinulenta*	common

OWLET MOTHS – continued

____	**Jocose Sallow**	*Feralia jocosa*	uncommon
____	**Ashen Pinion**	*Lithophane antennata*	common
____	**Grote's Pinion**	*Lithophane grotei*	common
____	**Nameless Pinion**	*Lithophane innominata*	common
____	**Dowdy Pinion**	*Lithophane unimoda*	common
____	**Figure-Eight Sallow**	*Psaphida resumens*	fairly common
____	**Mustard Sallow**	*Pyreferra hesperidago*	fairly common
____	**Bicolored Sallow**	*Sunira bicolorago*	common
____	no common name	*Sutyna privata*	uncommon

Subfamily Amphipyrinae {34}

____	**Elder Shoot Borer Moth**	*Achatodes zeae*	fairly common
____	**Doubtful Agroperina**	*Agroperina dubitans*	fairly common
____	**American Ear Moth**	*Amphipoea americana*	fairly common
____	**Veiled Ear Moth**	*Amphipoea velata*	uncommon
____	**Copper Underwing**	*Amphipyra pyramidoides*	abundant
____	**The Mouse**	*Amphipyra tragopoginis*	uncommon
____	**The Slowpoke**	*Anorthodes tarda*	abundant
____	**Yellow-headed Cutworm Moth**	*Apamea amputatrix*	fairly common
____	**White-blotched Balsa**	*Balsa labecula*	fairly common
____	**Three-lined Balsa**	*Balsa tristrigella*	fairly common
____	**Pink-shaded Fern Moth**	*Callopistria mollissima*	fairly common
____	**Cloaked Marvel**	*Chytonix palliatricula*	common
____	**Glassy Cutworm Moth**	*Crymodes devastator*	fairly common
____	**Festive Midget**	*Elaphria festivoides*	common
____	**American Angle Shades**	*Euplexia benesimilis*	fairly common
____	**The Wedgling**	*Galgula partita*	common
____	**Common Hyppa**	*Hyppa xylinoides*	fairly common
____	**Gray Half-Spot**	*Nedra ramosula*	common
____	**Common Pinkband**	*Ogdoconta cinereola*	common
____	no common name	*Oligia exhausta*	fairly common
____	**Black-banded Brocade**	*Oligia modica*	fairly common
____	**Northern Burdock Borer Moth**	*Papaipema arctivorens*	fairly common
____	**Burdock Borer Moth**	*Papaipema cataphracta*	fairly common
____	**Ironweed Borer Moth**	*Papaipema cerussata*	uncommon
____	**Stalk Borer Moth**	*Papaipema nebris*	fairly common
____	no common name	*Papaipema rutila*	fairly common
____	**Red Groundling**	*Perigea xanthioides*	occasional
____	**Brown Angle Shades**	*Phlogophora periculosa*	fairly common
____	**Spotted Phosphila**	*Phosphila miselioides*	fairly common
____	**Turbulent Phosphila**	*Phosphila turbulenta*	fairly common
____	**Dusky Groundling**	*Platysenta vecors*	fairly common
____	**Miranda Moth**	*Proxenus miranda*	fairly common
____	**Fall Armyworm Moth**	*Spodoptera frugiperda*	common
____	**Yellow-striped Armyworm Moth**	*Spodoptera ornithogalli*	fairly common

Subfamily Agaristinae {3}

____	**Eight-spotted Forester**	*Alypia octomaculata*	common
____	**Beautiful Wood-Nymph**	*Eudryas grata*	fairly common
____	**Pearly Wood-Nymph**	*Eudryas unio*	occasional

Subfamily Heliothinae {4}

____	**Spotted Straw**	*Heliothis turbatus*	uncommon
____	**Corn Earworm Moth**	*Heliothis zea*	common
____	**Lynx Flower Moth**	*Schinia lynx*	uncommon
____	**Ragweed Flower Moth**	*Schinia rivulosa*	common

Subfamily Acontiinae {10}

____	**Tufted Bird-Dropping Moth**	*Cerma cerintha*	common

AMPHIBIANS of Somerset County, PA

General:

Amphibians are defined as cold-blooded vertebrates with gilled, aquatic larvae. At least one time in their life, most amphibians are dependent on water in which to live. Those that do not require a watery medium still must have relatively constant moisture to keep their skin from drying out since amphibians are usually smooth, glossy, and moist – a notable exception being toads that are dry and bumpy. Most toad species are found actively hopping about places far from water and breathing with lungs, but they at one point were tadpoles with gills to which water was essential.

Reptiles, on the other hand, mostly have dry, rough, or scaly skin. The majority of them are not dependent on a moist or watery medium, and there are no larval stages.

Some salamanders have lungs, some have gills, and some obtain oxygen through "cutaneous respiration" as adults and have no lungs *or* gills. So their skin must then stay moist to aid in gas exchange. The **red-spotted newt** starts as a gill-breather and then undergoes a transformation to the lung-breathing, land-dwelling **"red eft"** before finally returning to the water as a greenish adult. All this being as it were, the amphibian hunter should focus on moist areas. But standing water is not essential for many species. Moist forest floors harbor lots of salamanders and the ubiquitous **redback salamander** is readily found anywhere damp. In fact, if there is enough wetness in your basement, they may even turn up there. The **longtail salamander** is another common cellar dweller. **Hellbenders,** on the other hand, are truly aquatic and live in rocky rivers. They're our largest salamander at over 1-½ feet.

We have only one toad species, the **American toad,** but Fowler's toad *(Bufo woodhousii fowleri)* occurs on all sides of us, and so should be watched for as it could turn up here. **Green frogs** are the classic pond frogs and **pickerel frogs** are often found along muddy ditches and shallow sloughs. **Bullfrogs** grow surprisingly large – sometimes over six inches – and will eat anything smaller than themselves, including snakes, turtles, baby birds, smaller frogs, fish and crayfish. **Mountain chorus frog** is becoming hard to find over all of its range; any sightings of this rarity should be reported to experts in the field.

Where & When:

Amazingly, salamanders can be looked for while ice still coats the waters. Looking for **spotted salamanders** at night in late March/early April is one of the rites of spring for enthusiasts. These large salamanders can be found easily only at this time of year: a flashlight and a few small ponds are all that's needed. Vernal pools (temporary pools in spring) are perhaps even better. If you can brave the cold, the similar **Jefferson salamander** actually emerges first in the same habitat. Most salamanders are nocturnal and so nighttime can be best for many of the difficult species. But lifting stones in a shallow woodland stream at high noon can be productive as well. Also, looking under big strips of bark or rotten logs in woodlands is a sure bet. [When looking for any type of creature, always remember to replace lifted items to their original spot.] Just as the salamanders emerge early, they fade away late and can be looked for into November. **Red-spotted newts** may be relatively active through the winter while under the ice.

Peepers time their spring chorus with the first real start of a thaw and are an aural delight for rural residents. It can be deafening to stand among a large population in full sway! Frogs may be identified easily by their calls. Tapes are available to this end at many nature-focused stores. **Spring peepers** are often frustratingly difficult to find at dusk even though they are singing. Given some time for nightfall, they become surprisingly simple to locate in a flashlight beam as they move out from under cover.

Facts & Figures:

➤ Increased frog deformities in the news are thought to be primarily the result of a parasite.

➤ Female frogs may release up to 30,000 eggs at one deposition.

➤ Metamorphosis from "pollywog" to frog or toad varies from as little as two months up to three years.

➤ **Pickerel frogs** have squarish blotches and yellow under the legs. **Leopard frogs** have round spots and white underlegs. In our county, **pickerel frogs** are much more common.

➤ Frogs partly freeze during winter hibernation; and some produce an antifreeze agent for cold endurance.

➤ There are virtually no residents of our county who've seen **green salamander** here in the wild. They occur in PA only in sandstone cliffs of Fayette and western Somerset Counties. Adding to the difficulty are a preference for deep rock cracks and a nocturnal habit.

➤ There is a nationwide decline among some amphibians that is not yet well understood. Locally, **leopard frogs** and **hellbenders** have undergone precipitous declines – partly from human activities.

➤ The pretty **slimy salamander** secretes a substance that makes it feel sticky to the touch.

AMPHIBIANS of Somerset County, PA

& Folklore:

➤ Toads do not cause warts. They do however, secrete a toxin – *bufotoxin* – that makes them un-tasty to would-be predators. You can see this milky solution being secreted if you look closely at a toad's skin. Fish will eat toad tadpoles and then promptly spit them back out as even the tadpole secretes bufotoxin. But the secretion does not trouble some predators; **hognose snakes** feed mostly on toads!

➤ Salamanders are not attracted to fire. It may seem that way when campfires are started and salamanders exit the collected wood or bark.

➤ **Hellbenders** are not dangerous or poisonous, but some fishermen fear them and cut lines rather than remove a hook when they catch them. Their large size and unusual appearance perpetuate this myth.

➤ Most "lizards" (reptiles) that are found here are really salamanders (amphibians). An old adage: if you were able to catch it . . . it probably wasn't a lizard.

Some Terms of Interest:

Amplexus	the mating embrace of frogs, toads, and newts
Arboreal	living in, or inhabiting trees
Bufotoxin	secreted by toads onto their skin, taste causes many predators to ignore them
Herpetology	the science or study of amphibians and reptiles; *herpetologists* study herps
"Herp"	slang for any given amphibian or reptile
Larva	the life stage emergent from the egg (*larvae* is plural)
Metamorphose Toads	tiny black toads that are found right after the tadpole becomes a toad
Neotenic	refers to larval characteristics retained in the adult stage
Oviparous	bearing eggs that develop <u>outside</u> the maternal parent
Tympanum	eardrum; easily visible on frogs

Activities:

• On the chapter list, check all of the amphibians that you have found. Make notes on where and when.

• Collect frog eggs and keep them for kids to witness the transformation to tadpoles. Remember that there are legal limits regarding possession of reptiles and amphibians – see www.pgc.state.pa.us.

• Create a terrarium: easily done with moss, peat, soil, moisture, and small vegetation. Add a salamander.

• *Always* replace rocks <u>first</u> and release herps afterwards to get back under cover – to avoid crushing them.

• Listen to ponds on spring evenings and learn the calls of frogs: peepers peep high and loud; **toads** have long trills; **bullfrogs** are bass foghorns or a "jug-o-rum"; and **green frogs** are the classic "twang" sound.

• Take your kids hunting for frogs along a pond's edge, or try catching tadpoles as well.

• Determine the gender of a frog: put a fly in front of it . . . if *he* eats it then it's a male, if *she* eats it then it's a female! [Truthfully, some frog species may be sexed by eardrum size in relation to the eye.]

• Catch a **spring peeper** or two and keep them overnight in a jar for kids to see. Slowly add cool water to the jar from the wetland where you collected them before release (to avoid temperature shock).

• The Northern Ohio Association of Herpetologists (N.O.A.H.) is an excellent source of information through its newsletter and other publications. Their address is: NOAH, Department of Biology, Case Western Reserve University, Cleveland, Ohio 44106. Check them out online at their website: www.noahonline.net/index.shtml and visit their sponsor www.kingsnake.com, which serves as an all-around online herpetology source as well. Or try the Pittsburgh Herpetological Society at: trfn.clpgh.org/phs.

County Status Codes:

Abundant	easily found in appropriate habitat, often in good numbers
Common	likely to be found in appropriate habitat
Fairly Common	usually able to find (with some effort); may be common but more secretive
Uncommon	requires a special effort or locale to find on demand, will be missed regularly
Occasional	difficult to find on demand in our county; not encountered much
Rare	has occurred in our county but even extensive searching may fail to locate
t	threatened in PA

Nomenclature follows that found in Hulse et al **(Sources)**. Genera and species appear alphabetically.

BIRDS of Somerset County, PA

General:

Birds comprise the class Aves: the hallmark of this class is *feathers* – all birds have them and they are unique to birds. Other traits are horny bills, air sacs for breathing, and pneumatic bones that are very light to aid flight. Many birds have more of their weight in feathers than in bones! The famed naturalist/artist Roger Tory Peterson believed that "birds are the most vivid expression of life" and for good reason. The diversity of function, form, and color among the winged is amazing in its breadth. Consider a **hummingbird, duck, falcon, heron, woodpecker,** and a **warbler** for a fine portrait of variability.

The majority of Somerset residents have no idea of the fascinating bird life that passes through our county. Birds like **loons, eagles,** and **sandpipers** are usually thought of as "elsewhere" by local residents but, in fact, are routine visitors. Better yet, *two* species of loons, *two* species of eagles, and over a *dozen* different sandpipers are regulars on the roster. And birds with unusual names like **scoter, avocet,** and **phalarope** present themselves on occasion as well. At this writing, 278 species have been documented in the county. Compare this number to the roughly 600 birds that are easily found in the entire continental U.S. and it is evident that we have a nice cross-section of birds represented locally. In any given year, observers can tally over 200 species without crossing our borders if they work at it. Bird watching, or "birding", has gained considerable momentum in recent years and the number of participants continues to swell. It is enjoyable at all levels: from the feeder watchers who have little idea of the identity of their patrons to the hard-core birders who revel in tracking down regional rarities.

We also boast a sizable list of nesting birds for the state that currently stands at 142 species. Somerset County sits along the southern border of the commonwealth but yet is the "roof garden" of PA; this provides for some interesting nesting combinations. **Golden-crowned Kinglet,** a resident of northern US and Canada, nests along our mountains: lowlands host the **Yellow-throated Warbler** – a bird of more southern haunts. One of the state's southernmost nesting outposts of **Hermit Thrush** is by the county line on Laurel Mountain. **Saw-whet Owl** (the owl on the license plates) nests at higher points locally. We have nesting **Ospreys, Upland Sandpipers,** and **Henslow's Sparrows**, which are all uncommon across Pennsylvania. Even the mid-western **Dickcissel** nested here during a recent invasion year.

Where & When:

Taking up "birding" as a hobby is a simple task. All you need is a pair of binoculars and a field guide; *Peterson's Guide* is excellent for both beginning and advanced birders. Very interesting birds can be found even in the middle of Somerset. In fact, two species – **Chimney Swift** and **Common Nighthawk** – are most easily found in urban areas. Beginners should focus on learning one bird at a time and not worry about the ones they can't identify. After mastering back yard birds, check out different habitats for other species. Birds have definite habitat preferences; so varying the type of environment you're in will maximize the number of bird species that you'll get to see and enjoy. Birding around lakes and stream thickets will likely net the most variety. Mornings are usually best, although any time of day can be productive. Dawn is when bird chorus is the loudest and this is especially true in May and June when nesting activity is at peak. Be warned . . . spotting birds with your binoculars can become addictive!

Some Terms of Interest:

Alternate Plumage	bird's feather garb during the breeding season; more colorful *(summer plumage)*
Basic Plumage	bird's feather garb during most of year; usually more plain (often *winter plumage*)
Big Day	a birder seeking as many species of birds as possible in a calendar day (in a given area)
Big Year	as in a Big Day, but in one calendar year
Empids	flycatcher group; "Empidonax" flycatchers' genus such as **Willow Flycatcher**
Fall-out	weather causes large numbers of migrants to appear; seemingly to drop out of the sky
"LBJ"	Little Brown Job; any nondescript small brownish birds, e.g., **sparrows, wrens**
Lifelist	a list kept to record all birds seen by an observer; sometimes kept competitively
Lifer	a bird found that is new to the observer; may be cause for celebration
Ornithology	the science of bird study; an *ornithologist* studies birds
Passerines	a group (an Order) of perching birds; the largest percentage of our birds are in this order
Peeps	slang for a group of small sandpipers (e.g., **Least Sandpiper**) for the call they make
Pishing	noise made to attract small birds; meant to imitate hawk; also called "spishing"
Raptors	birds of prey: **hawks, eagles, falcons,** and **owls** – some include **vultures** and **shrikes**
Squeaking	noise made to attract birds; kissing the back of your hand to imitate a distressed animal

BIRDS of Somerset County, PA

Facts & Figures:

➤ Represented here are 278 bird species in 18 orders and 51 families of birds; 142+ species nest locally.

➤ Baby birds on the ground are often part of the fledging process and should *not* be taken inside.

➤ Baby birds require intense amounts of care – let their parents do that. Simply keep the cats away.

➤ Passage time for ingesta is quite short: as little as 20 minutes sometimes. Birds have no teeth, but a muscular *gizzard* grinds the food before it enters the stomach. The *crop* is simply an esophageal pouch allowing birds to store more food than they can process. That is of most importance to birds that feed only a couple times per day such as a grouse.

➤ **Barn Swallows** migrate from the barns around here to South America each fall and the same birds return to the same locales in April. It is estimated that they fly about 600 miles on some days while *here*.

➤ **White Pelican's** wing span may exceed nine feet (~ floor to bottom of basketball net); they are huge.

➤ **Mute Swans** may sometimes weigh in the neighborhood of 50 pounds (typically ~20); achieving flight at that weight is a phenomenal task and takes a lot of effort (large eagles weigh between 10-15 pounds).

➤ **Hummingbirds,** on the other hand, weigh about as much as a penny. These little dynamos pump their wings roughly 50-75 times *per second* and their heart rate hits 1200 beats per minute in flight!

➤ Ancients thought birds flew to the moon in the winter. They don't go that high, of course, but birds often fly at altitudes of over 10,000 feet in migration (close to two miles high).

➤ Many of our **"diving" ducks** can go to depths of 100 feet (light fades out around 100 feet). But **loons** have become ensnared in netting below 200 feet where the pressure is considerable! As a point of reference, the Somerset County Courthouse is 135 feet tall to the tip of the vane; and utility poles are typically about 35-40 feet in height. **Loons** are agile swimmers and may stay submerged for as much as *15 minutes* in some cases, although less than a minute is more typical.

➤ **Falcons** are credited as the fastest birds: **Peregrines** have been recorded at over 200 mph in a stoop or dive. Next time that you're travelling at 65 mph, look out the window and imagine a bird doing triple that figure. **Racing pigeons** can go 94 mph in straight flight; **ducks** range from 40 – 60 mph average flight speed, and the small perching birds usually clock between 20 – 30 mph on the wing.

➤ Most of our local perching birds incubate eggs for about 10 – 20 days; two weeks is typical. They usually lay one egg per day, and most females don't start incubating until the clutch is complete.

Some Bird Nicknames:

"Baldpate"	**American Wigeon**
"Bluebill"	any of **Scaup, Ring-neck Duck**
"Bog-Pumper"	**American Bittern**
"Thunder Pumper"	**American Bittern**
"Butcher-bird"	either **Loggerhead** or **Northern Shrikes**
"Chewink"	**Eastern Towhee**
"Goastsucker"	any of a family of birds including **Nighthawk & Whip-poor-will**
"Jenny Wren"	**House Wren**
"Rain Crow"	**Black-billed** or **Yellow-billed Cuckoo**
"Shite Poke"	**Green Heron**
"Fly-Up-The-Creek"	**Green Heron**
"Snowbird"	any of **Snow Bunting, Junco, Longspur, or Horned Lark**
"Buzzard"	usually refers to **vulture** in the U.S.; a hawk in Europe
"Sparrow Hawk"	**American Kestrel**
"Pigeon Hawk"	**Merlin**
"Duck Hawk"	**Peregrine Falcon**
"Chicken Hawk"	any large hawk – usually **Red-tailed Hawk**
"Marsh Hawk"	**Northern Harrier**
"Fish Hawk"	**Osprey**
"Timberdoodle"	**American Woodcock**
"Yellowhammer"	**Common Flicker**

BIRDS of Somerset County, PA

Activities:

- On the chapter list, check all of the birds that you have found. Make notes on where and when.
- Go birding: on a walk with friends, alone near your home, at the park, or near a lake.
- Buy tapes of bird songs and calls; play them while driving to and from work. The benefits of knowing these songs when birding in the field are hard to overstate.
- Feeding birds is a national pastime and can draw in plenty of unusual species to observe. The science of feeding birds can be mystifying to beginners with all the different feeders and feeds available but really distills to a few basic approaches. My wife and I simply put out a couple different kinds of feeders to sate our avian entertainers. We put mixed seed in traditional feeders, thistle seed in finch feeders, suet in suet feeders, sugar in **hummingbird** feeders [4 parts water/1 part sugar; boil, chill & serve], a "shelf" feeder with just sunflower seed and occasionally slices of oranges in spring to draw in orioles. Keep the feeders clean to avoid causing disease.
- Watch the large lakes in the county during March/April and November. Bad weather will populate them with large numbers and a great variety of birds. Twenty-one species of **duck** have been observed in a weekend and groups of 400 – 500 **Tundra Swans** may alight for awhile. Over 100 **Common Loons** (*and* up to four **Red-throated Loons**) have visited Lake Somerset at once. Sea ducks visit occasionally.
- Birdhouses can be lots of fun as well. Even birds such as **screech owls** and **kestrels** can be attracted to appropriate nest boxes and there are plenty of books regarding house types. Build your own or buy them.
- The Allegheny Front Hawkwatch is located in Bedford County within shouting distance of the Somerset County line. It's a "can't miss" and is excellent for **eagles, hawks,** and **falcons** (directions in **Appendix**).
- Join a local or national bird club. *Pennsylvania Birds* is a quarterly journal published by the Pennsylvania Society for Ornithology and focuses on birds in the commonwealth. Nationally, the American Birding Association is an outstanding organization that caters to those who are interested in birds and birding. The local Allegheny Plateau Audubon Society is a thriving all-around conservation group ready and willing to help newcomers. With them, you may learn about birds and many other wild things.

Pennsylvania Birds
www.pabirds.org
P.O. Box 12823
Reading, PA 19612
Phone: (610) 372-3671
Email: kknight@epix.net

American Birding Association
www.americanbirding.org
ABA, PO Box 6599, Colorado Springs, CO 80934, USA
Phone: (719) 578-9703 Fax: (719) 578-1480
Email: member@aba.org

Allegheny Plateau Audubon Society
www.geocities.com/alleghenyplateau
Email: wetmeadow@aol.com

County Status Codes:

W – Winter	December – February
Sp – Spring	March – May
Su – Summer	June – July
F – Fall	August – November

The birds are listed below in phylogenetic order as found in McWilliams & Brauning. Nomenclature also follows that reference.

a – abundant: observable in large numbers in suitable habitat
c – common: should be seen during much of the season in suitable habitat
fc – fairly common: reliably present, but may be difficult to locate at times
u – uncommon: present all or part of season, but often not easily found or very secretive
o – occasional: reported only a few times in the season – some seasons not at all
r – rare: not seen every year, may be only a handful of records
x – extremely rare or **accidental:** one or few records, may not occur again for years
* confirmed breeding species in county either currently or in recent past
^^ breeding is probable
e   endangered in PA (9)   *e*✱ = Federal Endangered Species List (1)
t   threatened in PA (5)
extirpated: formerly occurred here and still does elsewhere / *extinct:* no longer occurs anywhere
[bird name in brackets] hypothetical occurrence (3 total): not officially counted for varied reasons

BIRDS of Somerset County, PA

Species: [278] Additions are likely, but relatively few.

Order Gaviiformes

LOONS – Family Gaviidae [2]

			W	Sp	S	F
____	**Red-throated Loon**	*Gavia stellata*	o	u	x	u
____	**Common Loon**	*Gavia immer*	u	c	x	c

Order Podicipediiformes

GREBES – Family Podicipedidae [3]

			W	Sp	S	F
____	**Pied-billed Grebe**	*Podilymbus podiceps*	o	c	o	c
____	**Horned Grebe**	*Podiceps auritus*	o	fc	-	fc
____	**Red-necked Grebe**	*Podiceps grisegena*	r	o	-	o
	[Western Grebe sp.]	*Aechmophorus occidentalis/clarkii*	-	-	-	x

Order Procellariiformes

SHEARWATERS & PETRELS – Family Procellariidae [1]

____	**Black-capped Petrel**	*Pterodroma hasitata*	-	-	-	x

Order Pelecaniformes

PELICANS – Family Pelecanidae [1]

____	**American White Pelican**	*Pelecanus erythrorhynchos*	-	x	-	-

CORMORANTS – Family Phalacrocoracidae [1]

____	**Double-crested Cormorant**	*Phalacrocorax auritus*	r	u	o	u

Order Ciconiiformes

BITTERNS & HERONS – Family Ardeidae [8]

			W	Sp	S	F
____ *e*	**American Bittern**	*Botaurus lentiginosus*	-	o	r	o
____ ^^*e*	**Least Bittern**	*Ixobrychus exilis*	-	r	r	-
____ *	**Great Blue Heron**	*Ardea herodias*	u	c	c	c
____ *e*	**Great Egret**	*Ardea alba*	-	u	o	u
____	**Snowy Egret**	*Egretta thula*	-	x	-	-
____	**Little Blue Heron**	*Egretta caerulea*	-	-	-	x
____ *	**Green Heron**	*Butorides virescens*	-	fc	fc	fc
____	**Black-crowned Night-Heron**	*Nycticorax nycticorax*	-	r	r	r

AMERICAN VULTURES – Family Cathartidae [2]

____	**Black Vulture**	*Coragyps atratus*	-	r	r	r
____ *	**Turkey Vulture**	*Cathartes aura*	-	c	c	c

Order Anseriformes

DUCKS, GEESE, & SWANS – Family Anatidae [33]

____	**Greater White-fronted Goose**	*Anser albifrons*	-	x	-	-
____	**Snow Goose**	*Chen caerulescens*	o	o	-	o
____	**Ross's Goose**	*Chen rossii*	-	-	-	x
____ *	**Canada Goose**	*Branta canadensis*	c	a	c	a
____	**Brant**	*Branta bernicla*	-	-	-	r
____ *	**Mute Swan**	*Cygnus olor*	-	r	r	r
	[Trumpeter Swan]	*Cygnus buccinator*	-	-	-	x
____	**Tundra Swan**	*Cygnus columbianus*	o	u	-	u
____ *	**Wood Duck**	*Aix sponsa*	o	c	c	c

BIRDS of Somerset County, PA

DUCKS, GEESE, & SWANS – continued		W	Sp	S	F
Gadwall	*Anas strepera*	o	fc	-	fc
Eurasian Wigeon	*Anas penelope*	-	x	-	x
American Wigeon	*Anas americana*	o	c	-	c
* American Black Duck	*Anas rubripes*	o	c	o	c
* Mallard	*Anas platyrhynchos*	c	a	c	a
* Blue-winged Teal	*Anas discors*	-	fc	o	fc
Cinnamon Teal	*Anas cyanoptera*	-	x	-	-
Northern Shoveler	*Anas clypeata*	-	u	-	u
Northern Pintail	*Anas acuta*	r	u	-	o
Green-winged Teal	*Anas crecca*	o	c	-	c
Canvasback	*Aythya valisineria*	o	u	-	u
Redhead	*Aythya americana*	o	u	-	u
Ring-necked Duck	*Aythya collaris*	u	c	-	c
Greater Scaup	*Aythya marila*	r	o	-	o
Lesser Scaup	*Aythya affinis*	u	c	-	c
Surf Scoter	*Melanitta perspicillata*	-	r	-	r
White-winged Scoter	*Melanitta fusca*	-	o	-	o
Black Scoter	*Melanitta nigra*	-	r	-	r
Oldsquaw / Long-tailed Duck	*Clangula hyemalis*	r	o	-	o
Bufflehead	*Bucephala albeola*	u	c	-	c
Common Goldeneye	*Bucephala clangula*	o	u	-	u
* Hooded Merganser	*Lophodytes cucullatus*	u	c	o	c
Common Merganser	*Mergus merganser*	o	u	r	u
Red-breasted Merganser	*Mergus serrator*	o	c	-	fc
Ruddy Duck	*Oxyura jamaicensis*	u	c	-	c

Order Falconiformes
OSPREYS, KITES, EAGLES, HARRIERS, & HAWKS – Family Accipitridae [11]

		W	Sp	S	F
*t Osprey	*Pandion haliaetus*	-	u	u	u
e Bald Eagle	*Haliaeetus leucocephalus*	-	o	-	o
ʌʌ Northern Harrier	*Circus cyaneus*	o	c	u	c
* Sharp-shinned Hawk	*Accipiter striatus*	fc	fc	fc	fc
* Cooper's Hawk	*Accipiter cooperii*	fc	fc	fc	fc
ʌʌ Northern Goshawk	*Accipiter gentilis*	o	o	r	o
* Red-shouldered Hawk	*Buteo lineatus*	o	u	u	u
* Broad-winged Hawk	*Buteo platypterus*	-	c	u	c
* Red-tailed Hawk	*Buteo jamaicensis*	c	c	c	c
Rough-legged Hawk	*Buteo lagopus*	u	o	-	o
Golden Eagle	*Aquila chrysaetos*	o	o	r	u

FALCONS – Family Falconidae [3]

		W	Sp	S	F
* American Kestrel	*Falco sparverius*	c	c	c	c
Merlin	*Falco columbarius*	-	o	-	o
e Peregrine Falcon	*Falco peregrinus*	r	r	-	o

Order Galliformes
PHEASANTS, GROUSE, & TURKEYS – Family Phasianidae [3]

		W	Sp	S	F
* Ring-necked Pheasant	*Phasianus colchicus*	fc	fc	fc	fc
* Ruffed Grouse STATE BIRD!	*Bonasa umbellus*	fc	fc	fc	fc
* Wild Turkey	*Meleagris gallopavo*	c	c	c	c

NEW WORLD QUAIL – Family Odontophoridae [1]

		W	Sp	S	F
ʌʌ Northern Bobwhite	*Colinus virginianus*	o	u	u	o

BIRDS of Somerset County, PA

Order Gruiformes
RAILS, GALLINULES, & COOTS – Family Rallidae [4]

			W	Sp	S	F
_____ *	Virginia Rail	_Rallus limicola_	-	o	o	o
_____ *	Sora	_Porzana carolina_	-	o	r	o
_____ *	Common Moorhen	_Gallinula chloropus_	-	r	r	-
_____	American Coot	_Fulica americana_	o	c	o	c

CRANES – Family Gruidae [1]

			W	Sp	S	F
_____	Sandhill Crane	_Grus canadensis_	x	x	-	-

Order Charadriiformes
PLOVERS – Family Charadriidae [4]

			W	Sp	S	F
_____	Black-bellied Plover	_Pluvialis squatarola_	-	o	-	o
_____	American Golden-Plover	_Pluvialis dominica_	-	r	-	o
_____	Semipalmated Plover	_Charadrius semipalmatus_	-	u	o	u
_____ *	Killdeer	_Charadrius vociferus_	r	c	c	c

STILTS & AVOCETS – Family Recurvirostridae [1]

			W	Sp	S	F
_____	American Avocet	_Recurvirostra americana_	-	-	-	x

SANDPIPERS & PHALAROPES – Family Scolopacidae [23]

			W	Sp	S	F
_____	Greater Yellowlegs	_Tringa melanoleuca_	-	u	o	u
_____	Lesser Yellowlegs	_Tringa flavipes_	-	fc	o	fc
_____	Solitary Sandpiper	_Tringa solitaria_	-	c	o	c
_____ *	Spotted Sandpiper	_Actitis macularia_	-	c	u	c
_____ *t	Upland Sandpiper	_Bartramia longicauda_	-	u	u	o
_____	Ruddy Turnstone	_Arenaria interpres_	-	r	-	r
_____	Red Knot	_Calidris canutus_	-	-	-	x
_____	Sanderling	_Calidris alba_	-	r	-	o
_____	Semipalmated Sandpiper	_Calidris pusilla_	-	u	o	u
_____	Western Sandpiper	_Calidris mauri_	-	-	-	r
_____	Least Sandpiper	_Calidris minutilla_	-	u	o	u
_____	White-rumped Sandpiper	_Calidris fuscicollis_	-	r	-	-
_____	Baird's Sandpiper	_Calidris bairdii_	-	-	-	r
_____	Pectoral Sandpiper	_Calidris melanotos_	-	fc	-	fc
_____	Dunlin	_Calidris alpina_	-	r	-	o
_____	Stilt Sandpiper	_Calidris himantopus_	-	-	-	x
_____	Buff-breasted Sandpiper	_Tryngites subruficollis_	-	-	-	x
_____	Short-billed Dowitcher	_Limnodromus griseus_	-	r	-	o
_____	Long-billed Dowitcher	_Limnodromus scolopaceus_	-	-	-	x
_____ *	Common Snipe	_Gallinago gallinago_	r	u	o	o
_____ *	American Woodcock	_Scolopax minor_	-	fc	u	u
_____	Wilson's Phalarope	_Phalaropus tricolor_	-	-	-	x
_____	Red-necked Phalarope	_Phalaropus lobatus_	-	-	-	x

JAEGERS, GULLS, & TERNS – Family Laridae [12]

			W	Sp	S	F
_____	Laughing Gull	_Larus atricilla_	-	x	-	-
_____	Franklin's Gull	_Larus pipixcan_	-	x	-	-
_____	Black-headed Gull	_Larus ridibundus_	-	x	-	-
_____	Bonaparte's Gull	_Larus philadelphia_	-	u	-	u
_____	Ring-billed Gull	_Larus delawarensis_	o	c	o	c
_____	Herring Gull	_Larus argentatus_	o	u	-	u
_____	Great Black-backed Gull	_Larus marinus_	-	x	-	-
_____	Black-legged Kittiwake	_Rissa tridactyla_	-	x	-	-

JAEGERS, GULLS, & TERNS – continued		W	Sp	S	F
____ Caspian Tern	*Sterna caspia*	-	u	-	u
____ e Common Tern	*Sterna hirundo*	-	o	-	o
____ Forster's Tern	*Sterna forsteri*	-	u	o	u
____ e Black Tern	*Childonias niger*	-	o	-	o

Order Columbiformes
PIGEONS & DOVES – Family Columbidae [2]

		W	Sp	S	F
____ * Rock Dove	*Columba livia*	a	a	a	a
____ * Mourning Dove	*Zenaida macroura*	a	a	a	a
Passenger Pigeon	*Ectopistes migratorius*	extinct			

Order Cuculiformes
CUCKOOS – Family Cuculidae [2]

		W	Sp	S	F
____ * Black-billed Cuckoo	*Coccyzus erythrophthalmus*	-	u	u	o
____ * Yellow-billed Cuckoo	*Coccyzus americanus*	-	u	u	r

Order Strigiformes
BARN OWLS – Family Tytonidae [1]

		W	Sp	S	F
____ * Barn Owl	*Tyto alba*	r	r	r	r

TYPICAL OWLS – Family Strigidae [7]

		W	Sp	S	F
____ * Eastern Screech-Owl	*Otus asio*	c	c	c	c
Gray Morph____ Red Morph____					
____ * Great Horned Owl	*Bubo virginianus*	c	c	c	c
____ Snowy Owl	*Nyctea scandiaca*	r	-	-	-
____ * Barred Owl	*Strix varia*	fc	fc	fc	fc
____ Long-eared Owl	*Asio otus*	r	r	-	r
____ e Short-eared Owl	*Asio flammeus*	o	r	-	o
____ * Northern Saw-whet Owl	*Aegolius acadicus*	o	o	o	o

Order Caprimulgiformes
GOATSUCKERS – Family Caprimulgidae [3]

		W	Sp	S	F
____ * Common Nightawk	*Chordeiles minor*	-	u	u	u
____ Chuck-will's-widow	*Caprimulgus carolinensis*	-	-	x	-
____ * Whip-poor-will	*Caprimulgus vociferus*	-	o	u	r

Order Apodiformes
SWIFTS – Family Apodidae [1]

		W	Sp	S	F
____ * Chimney Swift	*Chaetura pelagica*	-	c	c	c

HUMMINGBIRDS – Family Trochilidae [2]

		W	Sp	S	F
____ * Ruby-throated Hummingbird	*Archilocus colubris*	-	c	c	c
____ Selasphorus sp. Hummingbird	*Selasphorus sp.*	-	-	x	-
(probable Rufous Hummingbird – *S. rufus*)					

Order Coraciiformes
KINGFISHERS – Family Alcedinidae [1]

		W	Sp	S	F
____ * Belted Kingfisher	*Ceryle alcyon*	o	c	c	c

BIRDS of Somerset County, PA

Order Piciformes

WOODPECKERS – Family Picidae [7]

			W	Sp	S	F
_____ *	**Red-headed Woodpecker**	_Melanerpes erythrocephalus_	r	o	o	o
_____ *	**Red-bellied Woodpecker**	_Melanerpes carolinus_	fc	fc	fc	fc
_____ *	**Yellow-bellied Sapsucker**	_Sphyrapicus varius_	o	u	o	u
_____ *	**Downy Woodpecker**	_Picoides pubescens_	c	c	c	c
_____ *	**Hairy Woodpecker**	_Picoides villosus_	fc	fc	fc	fc
_____ *	**Northern Flicker**	_Colaptes auratus_	o	c	c	c
_____ *	**Pileated Woodpecker**	_Dryocopus pileatus_	u	u	u	u

Order Passeriformes ("Perching Birds")

FLYCATCHERS – Family Tyrannidae [10]

			W	Sp	S	F
_____	**Olive-sided Flycatcher**	_Contopus cooperi_	-	r	-	r
_____ *	**Eastern Wood-Pewee**	_Contopus virens_	-	c	c	u
_____ t	**Yellow-bellied Flycatcher**	_Empidonax flaviventris_	-	o	r	o
_____ *	**Acadian Flycatcher**	_Empidonax virescens_	-	fc	fc	o
_____ *	**Alder Flycatcher**	_Empidonax alnorum_	-	o	u	-
_____ *	**Willow Flycatcher**	_Empidonax traillii_	-	u	c	o
_____ *	**Least Flycatcher**	_Empidonax minimus_	-	u	u	o
_____ *	**Eastern Phoebe**	_Sayornis phoebe_	o	c	c	c
_____ *	**Great Crested Flycatcher**	_Myiarchus crinitus_	-	fc	fc	u
_____ *	**Eastern Kingbird**	_Tyrannus tyrannus_	-	fc	fc	u

SHRIKES – Family Laniidae [2]

			W	Sp	S	F
_____ e	**Loggerhead Shrike**	_Lanius ludovicianus_	_extirpated_			
_____	**Northern Shrike**	_Lanius excubitor_	r	-	-	-

VIREOS – Family Vireonidae [6]

			W	Sp	S	F
_____ *	**White-eyed Vireo**	_Vireo griseus_	-	u	u	o
_____ *	**Yellow-throated Vireo**	_Vireo flavifrons_	-	u	u	o
_____ *	**Blue-headed Vireo**	_Vireo solitarius_	-	fc	u	fc
_____ *	**Warbling Vireo**	_Vireo gilvus_	-	o	o	-
_____	**Philadelphia Vireo**	_Vireo philadelphicus_	-	r	-	o
_____ *	**Red-eyed Vireo**	_Vireo olivaceus_	-	a	a	c

JAYS & CROWS – Family Corvidae [3]

			W	Sp	S	F
_____	**[Gray Jay]**	_Perisoreus canadensis_	x	-	-	-
_____ *	**Blue Jay**	_Cyanocitta cristata_	c	a	c	a
_____ *	**American Crow**	_Corvus brachyrhyncos_	a	a	a	a
_____ *	**Common Raven**	_Corvus corax_	u	u	u	u

LARKS – Family Alaudidae [1]

			W	Sp	S	F
_____ *	**Horned Lark**	_Eremophila alpestris_	c	c	fc	fc

SWALLOWS – Family Hirundinidae [6]

			W	Sp	S	F
_____ *	**Purple Martin**	_Progne subis_	-	r	r	o
_____ *	**Tree Swallow**	_Tachycineta bicolor_	-	c	c	u
_____ *	**Northern Rough-winged Swallow**	_Stelgidopteryx serripennis_	-	fc	o	fc
_____ *	**Bank Swallow**	_Riparia riparia_	-	fc	o	fc
_____ *	**Cliff Swallow**	_Petrochelidon pyrrhonota_	-	fc	fc	fc
_____ *	**Barn Swallow**	_Hirundo rustica_	-	a	a	c

BIRDS of Somerset County, PA

		W	Sp	S	F
CHICKADEES & TITMICE – Family Paridae [3]					
____ Carolina Chickadee	*Poecile carolinensis*	x	x	x	x
____ * **Black-capped Chickadee**	*Poecile atricapillus*	a	a	c	a
____ * **Tufted Titmouse**	*Baeolophus bicolor*	c	c	c	c
NUTHATCHES – Family Sittidae [2]					
____ ^^ **Red-breasted Nuthatch**	*Sitta canadensis*	o	o	r	o
____ * **White-breasted Nuthatch**	*Sitta carolinensis*	c	c	c	c
CREEPERS – Family Certhiidae [1]					
____ * **Brown Creeper**	*Certhia americana*	u	u	o	u
WRENS – Family Troglodytidae [6]					
____ * **Carolina Wren**	*Thyrothorus ludovicianus*	u	u	u	u
____ **Bewick's Wren**	*Thyromanes bewickii*	extirpated			
____ * **House Wren**	*Troglodytes aedon*	-	c	c	u
____ * **Winter Wren**	*Troglodytes troglodytes*	o	u	o	u
____ *t* **Sedge Wren**	*Cistothorus platensis*	-	-	r	-
____ **Marsh Wren**	*Cistothorus palustris*	-	r	-	-
KINGLETS – Family Regulidae [2]					
____ * **Golden-crowned Kinglet**	*Regulus satrapa*	fc	u	o	u
____ **Ruby-crowned Kinglet**	*Regulus calendula*	o	fc	-	fc
GNATCATCHERS – Family Sylviidae [1]					
____ * **Blue-gray Gnatcatcher**	*Polioptila caerulea*	-	c	c	u
THRUSHES – Family Turdidae [7]					
____ * **Eastern Bluebird**	*Sialia sialis*	u	c	c	c
____ * **Veery**	*Catharus fuscescens*	-	fc	u	u
____ **Gray-cheeked Thrush**	*Catharus minimus*	-	r	-	r
____ **Swainson's Thrush**	*Catharus ustulatus*	-	u	-	u
____ * **Hermit Thrush**	*Catharus guttatus*	r	u	u	u
____ * **Wood Thrush**	*Hylocichla mustelina*	-	c	c	r
____ * **American Robin**	*Turdus migratorius*	u	a	a	a
MOCKINGBIRDS, THRASHERS, & ALLIES – Family Mimidae [3]					
____ * **Gray Catbird**	*Dumetella carolinensis*	r	c	c	a
____ * **Northern Mockingbird**	*Mimus polyglottos*	r	u	u	o
____ * **Brown Thrasher**	*Toxostoma rufum*	-	fc	fc	u
STARLINGS – Family Sturnidae [1]					
____ * **European Starling**	*Sturnus vulgaris*	a	a	a	a
PIPITS – Family Motacillidae [1]					
____ **American Pipit**	*Anthus rubescens*	r	o	-	o
WAXWINGS – Family Bombycillidae [2]					
____ **Bohemian Waxwing**	*Bombycilla garrulus*	x	-	-	-
____ * **Cedar Waxwing**	*Bombycilla cedrorum*	u	c	c	c

BIRDS of Somerset County, PA

WOOD-WARBLERS – Family Parulidae [37]

			W	Sp	S	F
____ *	Blue-winged Warbler	*Vermivora pinus*	-	u	o	u
____ *	Golden-winged Warbler	*Vermivora chrysoptera*	-	u	u	u
____	Tennessee Warbler	*Vermivora peregrina*	-	u	-	u
____	Orange-crowned Warbler	*Vermivora celata*	-	r	-	r
____ *	Nashville Warbler	*Vermivora ruficapilla*	-	fc	o	fc
____ *	Northern Parula	*Parula americana*	-	fc	fc	fc
____ *	Yellow Warbler	*Dendroica petechia*	-	a	a	o
____ *	Chestnut-sided Warbler	*Dendroica pensylvanica*	-	c	c	c
____ *	Magnolia Warbler	*Dendroica magnolia*	-	fc	fc	fc
____	Cape May Warbler	*Dendroica tigrina*	-	u	-	fc
____ *	Black-throated Blue Warbler	*Dendroica caerulescens*	-	fc	fc	fc
____	Yellow-rumped Warbler / "Myrtle Warbler"	*Dendroica coronata*	o	c	-	c
____ *	Black-throated Green Warbler	*Dendroica virens*	-	c	c	c
____ *	Blackburnian Warbler	*Dendroica fusca*	-	fc	fc	fc
____ ^^	Yellow-throated Warbler	*Dendroica dominica*	-	o	o	-
____ *	Pine Warbler	*Dendroica pinus*	-	u	o	u
____ e✳	Kirtland's Warbler	*Dendroica kirtlandii*	-	-	-	x
____ *	Prairie Warbler	*Dendroica discolor*	-	u	o	u
____	Palm Warbler	*Dendroica palmarum*	-	u	-	u
____	Bay-breasted Warbler	*Dendroica castanea*	-	u	-	fc
____	Blackpoll Warbler	*Dendroica striata*	-	u	-	u
____ *	Cerulean Warbler	*Dendroica cerulea*	-	o	o	o
____ *	Black-and-White Warbler	*Mniotilta varia*	-	c	c	c
____ *	American Redstart	*Setophaga ruticilla*	-	c	c	c
____ ^^	Prothonotary Warbler	*Protonotaria citrea*	-	r	r	-
____ *	Worm-eating Warbler	*Helmitheros vermivorus*	-	o	o	o
____ *	Ovenbird	*Seiurus aurocapillus*	-	c	c	c
____ *	Northern Waterthrush	*Seiurus noveboracensis*	-	u	o	u
____ *	Louisiana Waterthrush	*Seiurus motacilla*	-	fc	fc	o
____ *	Kentucky Warbler	*Oporornis formosus*	-	u	u	u
____	Connecticut Warbler	*Oporornis agilis*	-	r	-	r
____ ^^	Mourning Warbler	*Oporornis philadelphia*	-	o	-	o
____ *	Common Yellowthroat	*Geothlypis trichas*	-	a	a	a
____ *	Hooded Warbler	*Wilsonia citrina*	-	c	c	u
____	Wilson's Warbler	*Wilsonia pusilla*	-	u	-	u
____ *	Canada Warbler	*Wilsonia canadensis*	-	u	u	u
____ *	Yellow-breasted Chat	*Icteria virens*	-	u	u	o

TANAGERS – Family Thraupidae [1]

			W	Sp	S	F
____ *	Scarlet Tanager	*Piranga olivacea*	-	c	c	c

NEW WORLD SPARROWS – Family Emberizidae [18]

			W	Sp	S	F
____ *	Eastern Towhee	*Pipilo erythrophthalmus*	r	a	a	a
____	American Tree Sparrow	*Spizella arborea*	fc	u	-	o
____ *	Chipping Sparrow	*Spizella passerina*	r	a	a	a
____	Clay-colored Sparrow	*Spizella pallida*	-	-	-	x
____ *	Field Sparrow	*Spizella pusilla*	o	c	c	c
____ *	Vesper Sparrow	*Pooecetes gramineus*	r	u	u	u
____ *	Savannah Sparrow	*Passerculus sandwichensis*	-	c	c	c
____ *	Grasshopper Sparrow	*Ammodramus savannarum*	-	c	c	fc
____ *	Henslow's Sparrow	*Ammodramus henslowii*	-	u	u	o
____	Fox Sparrow	*Passerella iliaca*	r	u	-	u
____ *	Song Sparrow	*Melospiza melodia*	u	a	a	a
____	Lincoln's Sparrow	*Melospiza lincolnii*	-	u	-	u

MAMMALS of Somerset County, PA

County Status Codes:

   The codes below wrestle with the problem of true abundance versus apparent abundance. For instance, **southern flying squirrels** are common, but most people see them only rarely due to the squirrel's nocturnal habits. Also, capture may be necessary to find and/or identify small mammals since some diagnostic features may only be observed in the hand; and thus they are difficult to recognize apart from those conditions.

Abundant	a mammal that is easily seen, and frequently seen without effort
Common	regularly encountered; may be truly abundant but not as readily observed
Fairly Common	possibly common, but not often observed; signs of presence more easily noted
Uncommon	may be common, but good effort (or capture) often needed to observe beast or sign
Occasional	either difficult to observe, scattered occurrence, low numbers, or capture necessary
Rare	very few in number or specialized local habitat; capture may be necessary to find

r	re-introduced (3) after having been extirpated (eliminated from this area)
i	introduced (3) and not native to this area
t or *e*	*t*hreatened (3) or *e*ndangered (1) in PA *e*✱ = Federal Endangered Species List (1)
Bats only:	HH=hibernates here (caves) MS=migrates south (tree bats) MT=migrates through

   Taxonomy follows Wilson and Reeder (1993). Alternate or former names are in parentheses. Genera and species appear alphabetically.

Species: [56] Additions are unlikely, but possible.

Order Didelphimorphia (Marsupialia) – Pouched Mammals

OPOSSUMS – Family Didelphidae [1]   **Status**

____	**Virginia Opossum**	*Didelphis virginiana*	common

Order Insectivora – Insect Eaters

SHREWS – Family Soricidae [7]

____		**Northern Short-tailed Shrew**	*Blarina brevicauda*	common
____	*e*	**Least Shrew**	*Cryptotis parva*	rare
____		**Masked Shrew**	*Sorex cinereus*	occasional
____		**Long-tailed (Rock) Shrew**	*Sorex dispar*	occasional
____		**Smoky Shrew**	*Sorex fumeus*	occasional
____		**Pygmy Shrew**	*Sorex hoyi*	uncommon
____	*t*	**West Virginia Water Shrew**	*Sorex palustris punctulatus*	rare

MOLES – Family Talpidae [2]

____	**Star-nosed Mole**	*Condylura cristata*	fairly common
____	**Hairy-tailed Mole**	*Parascalops breweri*	fairly common

Order Chiroptera – Bats

PLAIN-NOSED BATS – Family Vespertilionidae [9]

____		**Big Brown Bat**	*Eptesicus fuscus*	HH	common
____		**Red Bat**	*Lasiurus borealis*	MS	uncommon
____		**Hoary Bat**	*Lasiurus cinereus*	MS	uncommon
____		**Silver-haired Bat**	*Lasionycteris noctivagans*	MT	occasional
____	*t*	**Eastern Small-footed Myotis**	*Myotis leibii*	HH	occasional
____		**Little Brown Myotis**	*Myotis lucifugus*	HH	common
____		**Northern (Long-eared) Myotis** / (Keen's)	*Myotis septentrionalis*	HH	uncommon
____	*e*✱	**Indiana Myotis**	*Myotis sodalis*	HH	rare
____		**Eastern Pipistrel**	*Pipistrellus subflavus*	HH	common

MAMMALS of Somerset County, PA

Order Lagomorpha – Pikas, Rabbits, and Hares   <u>Status</u>
RABBITS & HARES – Family Leporidae [3]

____ *r*	**Snowshoe Hare**	*Lepus americanus*	rare
____	**Appalachian Cottontail**	*Sylvilagus obscurus*	rare
____	**Eastern Cottontail**	*Sylvilagus floridanus*	abundant

Order Rodentia – Gnawing Mammals
SQUIRRELS – Family Sciuridae [6]

____	**Southern Flying Squirrel**	*Glaucomys volans*	common
____	**Woodchuck / Groundhog**	*Marmota monax*	abundant
____	**Gray Squirrel**	*Sciurus carolinensis*	abundant
____	**Eastern Fox Squirrel**	*Sciurus niger <u>vulpinus</u>*	common
____	**Rufous-bellied Fox Squirrel____**	*Sciurus niger <u>rufiventer</u>*	occasional
____	**Eastern Chipmunk**	*Tamias striatus*	abundant
____	**Red Squirrel**	*Tamiasciurus hudsonicus*	abundant

BEAVERS – Family Castoridae [1]

____	**Beaver**	*Castor canadensis*	fairly common

RATS & MICE – Family Muridae (including former Cricetidae) [10]

____	**Southern Red-backed Vole**	*Clethrionomys gapperi*	uncommon
____ *t*	**Allegheny (Eastern) Woodrat**	*Neotoma magister (floridana)*	rare
____	**Meadow Vole**	*Microtus pennsylvanicus*	common
____	**Woodland Vole**	*Microtus pinetorum*	uncommon
____ *i*	**House Mouse**	*Mus musculus*	common
____	**Muskrat**	*Ondatra zibethicus*	common
____	**White-footed Mouse**	*Peromyscus leucopus*	common
____	**Deer Mouse**	*Peromyscus maniculatus*	common
____ *i*	**Norway Rat**	*Rattus norvegicus*	abundant
____	**Southern Bog Lemming**	*Synaptomys cooperi*	rare

JUMPING MICE – Family Dipodidae (Zapodidae) [2]

____	**Woodland Jumping Mouse**	*Napaeozapus insignis*	uncommon
____	**Meadow Jumping Mouse**	*Zapus hudsonius*	uncommon

NEW WORLD PORCUPINES – Family Erethizontidae [1]

____	**Porcupine**	*Erethizon dorsatum*	uncommon

Order Carnivora – Flesh Eaters
WOLVES, FOXES, & COYOTES – Family Canidae [3]

____	**Coyote**	*Canis latrans*	fairly common
____	**Gray Fox**	*Urocyon cinereoargenteus*	fairly common
____ *i*	**Red Fox**	*Vulpes vulpes*	fairly common

BEARS – Family Ursidae [1]

____	**Black Bear**	*Ursus americanus*	fairly common

RACCOONS – Family Procyonidae [1]

____	**Raccoon**	*Procyon lotor*	common

MAMMALS of Somerset County, PA

WEASELS, SKUNKS, BADGERS, OTTERS & ALLIES – Family Mustelidae [6]

			Status
____ r	River Otter	*Lontra (Lutra) canadensis*	rare
____	Striped Skunk	*Mephitis mephitis*	common
____ r	Fisher	*Martes pennanti*	occasional
____	Long-tailed Weasel	*Mustela frenata*	uncommon
____	Least Weasel	*Mustela nivalis*	uncommon
____	Mink	*Mustela vison*	uncommon

CATS – Family Felidae [1]

____	Bobcat	*Felis (Lynx) rufus*	occasional

Order Artiodactyla – Even-toed Hoofed Mammals
DEER – Family Cervidae [1]

____	White-tailed Deer	*Odocoileus virginianus*	abundant

Order Primates – Man, Apes, Monkeys & relatives
MAN – Family Hominidae [1]

____	Human !	*Homo sapiens*	abundant

Reviewed by:

James A. Hart – Mammalogist / Zoologist, The Nature Conservancy
Joseph F. Merritt, Ph.D. – Director, Powdermill Biological Station – Carnegie Museum of Natural History
Daniel W. Jenkins, Scott W. Tomlinson – Wildlife Conservation Officers, Pennsylvania Game Commission

Sources:

Alt, Gary. 1991. Video – *On the Trail of Pennsylvania's Black Bears*, The PA Game Commission.
Burt, William H. 1980. *A Field Guide to the Mammals (North America north of Mexico)*, Houghton Mifflin Co., Boston. 289 pp.
Felbaum, Frank. 1995. *Endangered and Threatened Species of Pennsylvania.* DCNR/WRCF, Harrisburg. 80 pp.
Merritt, Joseph F. 1987. *Guide to the Mammals of Pennsylvania.* University of Pittsburgh Press (Carnegie Museum of Natural History), Pittsburgh. 408 pp.
Whitaker, John O. Jr. 1980. *The Audobon Society Field Guide to North American Mammals*, Alfred A. Knopf, New York. 745 pp.
Whitaker, John O. Jr. and William J. Hamilton, Jr. 1998. *Mammals of the Eastern United States.* Cornell University Press, Ithaca. 583 pp.
Wilson, Don E. and DeeAnn M. Reeder. 1993. *Mammal Species of the World: A Taxonomic and Geographic Reference.* Smithsonian Institution, Washington, D.C. 1206 pp.

140

The following organisms are more easily found in the field than they are on the nature guide shelves of bookstores. Lay guides and literature are difficult to locate, but persistence will pay off if a person is intent on learning more. With the burgeoning interest in nature today, eventually there may be comprehensive field manuals for all of these engaging plants and creatures. As more becomes known of these organisms' distributions, more thorough coverage of species occurrence will be possible.

Slime molds cause problems for taxonomists because they combine aspects of both flora and fauna in their biology. They resemble fungi, but have the ability to move from place to place. Watch for their gooey presence on fallen logs in the woods or on the ground.

Studies are underway to catalogue the mosses and lichens found in the commonwealth – only a few of the many are mentioned here. **British soldiers**, an attractive lichen, is one of the more common examples in the county and often illustrated in general guidebooks or encyclopedias. Lichens are actually a symbiotic combination of an alga and a fungus, typically found growing on rocks or wood ("Freddy fungus took a lichen [likin'] to Allison algae and ever since their marriage has been on the rocks"). Beatrix Potter, who authored children's books about Peter Rabbit, first proposed the idea of lichens as symbiotic associations of two different organisms. She also spent much time studying and drawing lichens. To see **British soldiers**, look for a cluster of small, gray, coral-like structures that have red caps on their tops: old wood and stumps are likely spots. Lichens are classified as *crustose* (crusty), *foliose* (leaf-like), or *fruticose* (shrubby) depending on their morphology, or appearance. There are more than 350 species of lichens documented from the commonwealth.

Mosses are, of course, very common and there are numerous species are found in wet areas all around the county. Like the **lichens,** over 350 **moss** species have been reported statewide.

Liverworts and **hornworts** lead mosslike lives and are often mistaken for mosses. The liverlike shape of some plants gives them their name. Around 115 species of liverwort are found in Pennsylvania.

Few people would guess that **jellyfish** might be found in our streams given that words such as "seashore" and "ocean" come quickly to mind by association. But this is one of the secrets that a stream trotter learns by seining for minnows: **jellyfish** are among the many strange creatures that may be lifted from the water in seine nets. For the same reasons, many folks are surprised to learn that we grow our own "sea"shells – a variety of **clam** or **mussel** species are native to local waters.

Crayfish are common in area streams and ponds. My family enjoys finding them even in the spring that travels through the basement of our business. Some "crawdads" produce burrows that exit like gopher holes a short distance from the streams and springs that they inhabit. The abundant and well-known **pillbugs** and **sowbugs** are other examples of crustaceans.

Is it a **millipede** or a **centipede?** Millipedes have more legs (milli = thousand, centi = hundred) that are often shorter and seem to project below the body. **Centipedes'** legs usually flare out to the side and are longer, heavier, and fewer than those of a **millipede.**

Below is a brief sampling of members of various phyla found in our county and not already covered in previous chapters. These and many more discrete species await your discovery.

Additional Species: [28] This list is an introductory one – just a few of the large number of actual species present from these phyla are listed.

Flora/Fungi

_____	**Wood-loving Lycogala**	*Lycogala epidendrum*	Phylum Myxomycota (Protoctista)
_____	**Many-headed Slime**	*Physarum polycephalum*	"
_____	**Chocolate Tube Slime**	*Stemonitis splendens*	"
_____	**Yellow-green Algae ("Green Ground Jelly")**		Phylum Chlorophyta (in Protoctista)
_____	**British Soldiers**	*Cladonia cristatella*	Phylum Ascomycota (in Fungi)
_____	**Reindeer Lichen**	*Cladonia rangiferina*	"
_____	**Toad Skin Lichen / Rock Tripe**	*Lasallia (Umbilicaria) papulosa*	"
_____	**Common Liverwort**	*Marchantia polymorpha*	Phylum Bryophyta (in Plantae)
_____	**Common Hornwort**	*Phaeoceros laevis*	"
_____	**White Cushion Moss**	*Leucobyrum glaucum*	"
_____	**Hair Cap Moss**	*Polytrichum commune*	"
_____	**Peat Moss / Sphagnum Moss**	*Sphagnum spp.*	"

ADDITIONAL SPECIES of Somerset County, PA

Fauna

____	**Moss Animal**	*Pectinatella magnifica*	Phylum Bryozoa
____	**Jellyfish**	*Craspedacusta sowerbii*	Phylum Cnidaria
____	**Cat / Dog Round Worms**	*Toxocara cati / canis*	Phylum Nematoda
____	**Tapeworms**	*Dipylidium spp. / Taenia spp.*	Phylum Platyhelminthes, class Cestoda
____	**Night Crawler**	*Lumbricus terrestris*	Phylum Annelida, class Oligochaeta
____	**Stream Leech**	*Erpobdella punctata*	Phylum Annelida, class Hirudinea
____	**Little Pond Snail**	*Amnicola limnosa*	Phylum Mollusca, class Gastropoda
____	a common snail	*Mesodon thyroidus*	Phylum Mollusca, class Gastropoda
____	**Pond Papershell**	*Utterbackia (Anodonta) imbecillis*	Phylum Mollusca, class Bivalvia
____	**Pill Bug**	*Armadillidium vulgare*	Phylum Arthropoda, class Crustacea
____	**Eastern Crayfish**	*Cambarus carinirostris*	Phylum Arthropoda, class Crustacea
____	a crayfish	*Orconectes obscurus*	Phylum Arthropoda, class Crustacea
____	**Millipedes**		Phylum Mandibulata, class Myriapoda
____	**Common Scutigera** (Centipede)	*Scutigera coleoptrata*	Phylum Mandibulata, class Myriapoda

Helpful Websites:

Top-notch site for Pennsylvania's twelve species of crayfish – complete with identification key:
    www.lhup.edu/~tnuttall/pennsylvania_crayfish_reference_.htm
Learn more about freshwater mussels at: courses.smsu.edu/mcb095f/gallery/Default.htm
Learn more about Pennsylvania's mosses and lichens at the DCNR website:
    www.dcnr.state.pa.us/pabs/bryophytes_and_lichens.htm
Earthworms are interesting creatures. See for yourself at: www.smartgardening.com/Worm%20_Facts.htm
Search the internet for more information on any of the above biota.

Sources:

Georgi, Jay R. 1985. *Parasitology for Veterinarians.* W. B. Saunders Co., Philadelphia. 344 pp.
Lincoff, Gary H. 1984. *The Audubon Society Field Guide to North American Mushrooms.* Alfred A. Knopf, New York. 926 pp.
Reid, George K. 1967. *Pond Life (A Golden Guide).* Golden Press, New York. 160 pp.
Shuttleworth, Floyd S., and Herbert Zim. 1967. *Non-flowering Plants (A Golden Guide).* Golden Press, New York. 160 pp.
Wernert, Susan J. (editor). 1982. *North American Wildlife.* Reader's Digest, Pleasantville, NY. 559 pp.

THE SKIES ABOVE US in Somerset County, PA

General:

Although a departure from organisms, people who enjoy nature often desire knowledge of both day and nighttime skies. Of value to the naturalist, having a handle on weather helps to better anticipate bird movements, fish biting, mammal activity, or mushroom blooming. And knowing the stars greatly aids nighttime navigation for birds and sailors alike. Nothing of this discussion is unique to Somerset County, but here in our boundaries is as good a place as any other to look upwards. While this treatment will only lightly scratch the surface, a brief introduction to weather watching and stargazing may spur more interest. Most people live and die without ever seeing for themselves Saturn's rings and Jupiter's moons. Yet those planets are bright to the naked eye many nights of the year and their features are easily viewed with inexpensive optics. Get out there!

DAYTIME

Clouds:

Cloud names seem confusing, but are quickly learned with a little effort. They are classified and named according to how they are formed. Rising air currents produce *cumulus* type clouds (piled on or accumulated). Layers of air that are cooled below their saturation point produce *stratus* type clouds (layered or sheet-like). Altitude is another part of classification (height of cloud base in parentheses): high (18,000+ ft), middle (7000 – 18,000 ft), low (surface to 7000 ft), and towering (span the heights). Various prefixes and suffixes are employed to specify the type.

A nice thing about studying clouds – they're readily found since their preferred habitat is just outside the door. So not much investment is needed to locate subjects to study. Also, many helpful guide books are available. Some of the basic cloud types are:

Cumulus: the "big or little puffies" of summer sky, mostly low base - may tower to 75,000 feet (14 miles)
Cumulonimbus: the "big puffies" that are part of storms, *thunderheads*, often flat-topped
Cirrus: anything with *cirrus* or *cirro* in it means "up high", all ice crystals, "thin wispies"
Altocumulus & Altostratus: middle clouds, medium high ("alto" singer) - dark puffies or broad flats
Stratus: solid gray sheets of a leaden sky, drizzle only, low clouds without much definition
Nimbostratus: rain production clouds (*nimbo* means rain), darker than **stratus,** "rain streaks"
Stratocumulus: a seeming nomenclature anomaly: combines both main types, irregular masses; the "strato" first indicates *low* – these clouds are similar to altocumulus, but fall in the low elevation range

There are frequently several types of clouds in the sky at once.

As you advance in cloud identification, you will notice that there is often a "cloud sequence" that accompanies either a cold front approach or a warm front approach. Watch the weather forecast on the news and see how it relates to what you see in the sky both before and after the forecast. Warm fronts move slower but may influence cloud formations 1000 miles ahead of them.

Another interesting activity is to operate a weather station of your own. With knowledge of clouds, a barometer, a thermometer, and a wind vane, the amateur meteorologist can do surprisingly well at local predictions. Also keep a rain gauge . . . if for no other reason than to compare notes with your neighbor or a friend over the hill. Falling barometers generally indicate advancing rainy weather (low pressure) and rising barometer readings indicate approaching fair weather (high pressure). If you *keep records* of all the data you accumulate, and analyze the trends, it'll all come together. You'll know you're getting fancy if you begin to use a sling psychrometer to measure and keep track of humidity.

Lightning:

Lightning strikes the earth on the average about nine times per second! Lightning is an awesome force in nature and can provide a majestic display from a safe haven. In an average year over 200 people die in the U.S. from a lightning strike, so choose your haven well. Stay away from water and trees in the open. In fact, stay away from open areas altogether and seek out low-lying spots if you cannot get indoors. The air temperature surrounding the strike zone is hotter than the surface of the sun but is extremely brief in duration and quite thin. When you see a bolt of lightning, count the seconds until you hear thunder and then divide by 5 to determine the distance, in miles, that the storm is away from you (speed of sound = 1 mile per 5 seconds). Thus, a 10-second delay between strike and sound indicates the storm is 2 miles away.

THE SKIES ABOVE US in Somerset County, PA

Sun:

There is a joke about tipping waiters: "never look directly into the sun." It's a fine tip indeed. An observer can only look safely at the sun *indirectly* as the sun's image shines on a piece of paper after passing through a lens of a binocular or scope (consult **Sources** for specifics) *or*, directly, through a special screen such as a welding mask with a rating of 14. When the setting sun is on the horizon and is fully red, brief glances may be cast to check for sunspots. The sun is about 93,000,000 miles away on average, and so light takes a little over eight minutes to reach us even though travelling at 186,000 miles per second!

WEATHER DATA

We live in what is considered to be a temperate, humid climate in Somerset County. The biggest factor that sets us apart from neighboring counties' weather is that we're positioned up on the Allegheny Plateau in between two mountain chains. Due to this, we get more snow and have colder winters than our neighbors to the east and west. Snow skiing is consequently a big sport in the region of the "frosty sons of thunder", as Somerset Countians have been dubbed.

Because of the tilt of the earth's axis by 23 ½ degrees and also the yearlong trek of the earth around the sun, the sun's rays strike directly on the earth differently at various times of the year. Contrary to common perception, the earth does not wobble on this axis during the change of seasons, but instead maintains the same 23 ½ degree tilt all the time. It is the orbit around the sun that makes the North Pole tilt *towards* the sun at one point (our summer) and *away* from the sun six months later (our winter). **Vernal Equinox** (spring) and **Autumnal Equinox** (fall) are the times when the sun's rays hit the equator at a 90-degree angle, as the sun appears directly over-head there. The **Summer** and **Winter Solstices** occur when the sun is directly over-head at 23 ½ degrees north of the equator (our summer) or 23 ½ degrees south of the equator (our winter).

Somerset County Weather Stats:

➤ The mean maximum temperature in July =   84° F.
➤ The mean minimum temperature in July =   60° F.
➤ The mean maximum temperature in January =   35° F.
➤ The mean minimum temperature in January =   18° F.
➤ We get approximately 42" of precipitation per year: including 60 - 66" of snow per year.
➤ We average 34 days per winter when at least one inch of snow is on the ground.
➤ The heaviest recorded one-day rainfall is **4.93 inches** at Confluence on October 16, 1954.
➤ **Frosts** have been recorded in both early June and late August.
➤ Many residents will recall the evening of Dec. 12, 2000 when Somerset County was buffeted by wind speeds of 50 mph through the night that gusted up to *80 mph,* qualifying as hurricane force winds.
➤ **Tornadoes** may be expected here at the rate of 1-5 tornadoes in any 10-year period. We have recorded tornadoes that registered F4 on the Fujita-Pearson Scale (a violent tornado with winds over 200 mph).

Facts & Figures:

➤ The weather for a geographic location dramatically impacts the biota that may be found there. Every organism on the face of the planet reacts to changes in this most powerful natural force on earth.
➤ **Northern lights (aurora borealis)** are rarely observed in our county. They occur over 60 miles up in the atmosphere! There is virtually no meteorological activity above 50 miles high.
➤ It takes more than one million **snow crystals** to cover a two-foot square area with ten inches of snow.
➤ **Snow crystals** are always *six-sided*. Microscopic study allows for understanding that no two are alike.
➤ **Frost** is formed in the same manner as **dew** (water vapor condensing), but at temperatures at or below freezing. Feathery patterns of frost on the window are from thawing and freezing over and again.
➤ You can check **weather forecasts** for our area at www.weather.com/weather/local/15501.
➤ **Rainbows** are usually seen in the east opposite a setting sun. "Double rainbows" are color reversed.
➤ Jet condensation trails (contrails) occur at many heights, but all are at temperatures below freezing.
➤ **Hailstones** have diameters greater than 1/5 inch (5mm): the maximum-recorded size is for a colossal stone weighing **1.67 pounds** with a **17.5-inch** circumference in Kentucky. Hail is known for damaging crops, and people have been hurt badly and even (rarely) killed by these ice rocks from the sky.
➤ **Global warming** is almost indisputable. The question is the cause. Is it a natural event or not?

NIGHTTIME

Many folks get frustrated right away by any attempt to learn the nighttime skies because they think they have to know something prior to looking. The truth is that all you need to do is look. Eventually you may wish to study magnitudes, declinations, spectral types and the like, but you need never have to learn these things in order to stargaze. Just look up. Every part of the sky has items of interest. A basic star chart or guidebook will help you figure out the patterns of some of the constellations: and look at some of the brighter "stars" to find planets. Notice that as sunny days give way to night that cumulus clouds usually disappear and are not seen in the night sky. Stratus clouds are often present after sunset.

A good approach: set small goals and learn a little at a time – "nothing spurs success like success." Studying the heavens for just a minute or two each night (you get cloudy nights off) yields remarkable progress over time. Try stargazing both in the evening and in the early morning to see different things. And check the skies in *all seasons*. Stars are best observed on dark nights; so avoid town if you can, as the lights interfere with your enjoyment. Binoculars and telescopes will add new dimensions to your study.

Facts & Figures:

➤ There are about 2000 stars visible to the naked eye on dark nights, and 6000 in the course of a year.
➤ Stars *do not* move with respect to each other (in our lifetimes), planets *do* move among the stars.
➤ Space is largely empty: if the dot at the end of this sentence were our sun, the nearest other star would be a similar dot ten miles away.
➤ A **meteor** flashes through the sky; a **meteorite** actually hits the ground (meteorite "mite" hit nearby).
➤ Astronomers give no credence to astrology (the attempt to predict the future through the stars).
➤ The **zodiac** is a group of 12 constellations that the sun "passes through" as the earth revolves around it.
➤ **Harvest Moon,** around the Autumnal Equinox, results from the moon rising only ~20 minutes later each night (vs. the normal of ~50) thereby providing moonlight early in the evening for a longer duration.
➤ The "dark side of the moon" is, of course, not always dark. But the moon rotates on its axis in about the same time it takes to revolve around the earth, so we always see just one hemisphere from earth.
➤ **Space debris** consists of tens of thousands of marble sized objects caught in orbit around the earth. Rocket booster releases and satellite activities are common sources of this orbital garbage.

Activities:

• A telescope is a good family investment. Save to get one and then use it often. Also good for humility checks: Franklin Roosevelt ended many days while president looking at stars to gain proper perspective.
• Get a blanket to lie upon, special friend or family, some hot cocoa or iced tea in a thermos (given the weather) and lie back on a grassy knoll to watch the stars twinkle.
• American Indians (as well as many other cultures) tested vision by looking at the 2nd star in the handle of the Big Dipper; it's actually two stars. Check and see how good *your* vision is.
• Watch the Somerset *Daily American* for Dennis Mammana's excellent, weekly **Stargazers** column.
• Check out the Amateur Astronomers Association of Pittsburgh at trfn.clpgh.org/aaap/aaap3.html.

Planets:

The following planets are visible with either the naked eye or with regular binocular magnification.
• **Saturn** is fairly bright and visible to naked eye; its *rings can be detected with 10x binocs* held very still (better with a small scope). It's not as bright as Jupiter, but still stands out. Don't miss this one!
• **Jupiter** is readily seen and bright to the naked eye; binoculars easily reveal four of *Jupiter's moons*! These four are visible (of 28 total) with low-power glass: **Io, Europa, Ganymede,** and **Callisto.** Galileo discovered their existence.
• **Venus** is the "morning star" and "evening star" depending on its cycle. It has phases like the earth's moon and so will appear as a crescent at times. **Venus** is very bright to the naked eye, fuzzy to the sight through binoculars or scope, and is often the brightest thing in the night sky.
• **Mars** is known as the *red planet,* but actually appears bright yellow-orange (perhaps a reddish tinge vs. the other stars and planets). Check newspaper listings for times and locations.
• **Mercury:** seen in the east sky just prior to sunrise or in the west just after sunset at certain times of the year; has phases like the earth's moon.

Stars & Constellations:

- **Big Dipper** (part of **Ursa Major** or "Big Bear"): most people are familiar with this group of stars. So use this as a sky benchmark and then learn all other constellations in terms of their position with respect to the Big Dipper. For example: the two "pointer stars" at the *end* of the Big Dipper (furthest from handle) make a line to **Polaris** (the **North Star**) which is the first star in the handle of the **Little Dipper**. Because we sit at about the 40th parallel of latitude, we can see all or most of the Big Dipper all year long and all night long. Any further south and we couldn't claim that.
- **Little Dipper** (part of **Ursa Minor** or "Little Bear"): follow the line from the Big Dipper's pointers past the Little Dipper to find the constellations **Cepheus** (house-shaped) and **Cassiopeia.**
- The tail of **Draco** the Dragon snakes between the two dippers. It is quickly found by remembering this.
- **Cassiopeia** (a big "W" in the night sky) opens up to the Little Dipper.
- **Gemini** is located by following a line made by the two *bottom* stars of the cup of the Big Dipper forward.
- **Boötes** is found by tracing a line *backward* from the first two handle stars in the Big Dipper.
- **Orion** is the king of winter constellations and very easily found once a mental image is gained of what to look for. Two well-known bright stars, **Betelgeuse** ("beetle-juice") and **Rigel** occur here. Orion's belt and sword are the centerpieces of the group and his sword contains the great nebula **M42**. Make the effort to learn Orion – it's hard to miss on any clear winter or early spring night.

Moon:

One of the crowning achievements of science in the history of humanity is to send a party to walk on the moon and then have them return safely home. Most people are familiar with how the moon creates ocean tides, but not many of us can name even one geographic feature of the moon that we glance at so commonly on clear evenings.

Here's a simple fix if you'd like to remedy that situation. In a waxing moon (full moon still to come) or a full moon, look with binoculars for a rough "Mickey Mouse" face mostly on the Moon's right side (see figure 8). With a little imagination, it's not too hard to find – two big ears on a round head with a large, white nose in it. Most of Mickey's upper face is the **Sea of Tranquility** (Apollo 11 landed here); his left cheek is the **Sea of Fecundity,** with the **Crater of Langrenus** as a white pimple on it. Mickey's right ear is the **Sea of Serenity.** The big crater at the bottom of the moon is the **Crater of Tycho.** For those of gifted imagination, try to see a "cat" on the side opposite Mickey.

There are plenty of other features easily learned with the help of books about the Moon, and binoculars. Small scopes are best for viewing the mountains and craters; it is actually too bright to study with many larger telescopes. If you're watching in spring or fall you should be alert for silhouettes of migrating birds to pass over the face of the Moon. The birds aren't hard to spot – you can often hear them as well. That line on the moon that separates light from dark is called the **Terminator.** Watch its movement over a couple hours' time.

Other Heavenly Objects:

There's lots more than just planets, stars and a moon up there (any veteran stargazer will feel this section leaves out too many).

- **The Milky Way** is our home galaxy and is easily visible on any dark, clear night. It's a "milky" belt or cloud that is composed of the light from billions of stars, and it spans the sky.
- **Andromeda** is a galaxy also known as M31 – *the most distant object visible to the naked eye* (2 million light years). The light that makes the image you see left those stars 2 million years ago and traveled through space at 186,000 *miles per second* all that time until it finally strikes your retina and is appreciated by you! Amazing, yes? Look below or around **Cassiopeia** to find it – it's just a small smudge of light from the billions of stars that comprise the galaxy.
- **M42:** look with binoculars at Orion's sword to see this awesome **nebula** – it's visible to the naked eye.
- **Meteors** are best after midnight (when we're at the forefront of earth hurtling through space at about 12 miles per second). Meteor showers are named for the constellations from which they appear to originate.
- Watch the skies on the evening of **August 12** (in any given year) to see the **Perseid Meteor Shower** when about 50 meteors per hour streak across the sky – great natural fireworks.

THE SKIES ABOVE US in Somerset County, PA

Reviewed by:

Kevin B. Baker – Supervisory Meteorologist, National Weather Service, Elko, NV
Dennis L. Mammana – SkyScapes (www.skyscapes.com)

Sources:

Chartrand, Mark R. 1991. *The Audubon Society Field Guide to the Night Sky.* Alfred A. Knopf, New York. 714 pp.

Keen, Richard A. 1992. *Skywatch East: A Weather Guide.* Fulcrum Publishing, Golden, Colorado. 204 pp.

Lehr, Paul E. 1975. *Weather (A Golden Guide).* Golden Press, New York. 160 pp.

Ludlum, David. 1991. *National Audubon Society Field Guide to North American Weather.* Alfred A. Knopf, New York. 655 pp.

Mayall, R. Newton, Margaret Mayall, and Jerome Wyckoff. 1985. *The Sky Observer's Guide (A Golden Guide).* Golden Press, New York. 160 pp.

Shultz, Charles H. 1999. *The Geology of Pennsylvania.* Pennsylvania Geological Survey & Pittsburgh Geological Society; DCNR, Harrisburg. 888 pp.

Yaworski, Michael. 1983. *Soil Survey of Somerset County Pennsylvania.* United States Department of Agriculture & Soil Conservation Service. 148 pp.

Figure 8 – Moon Geography (see chapter text)

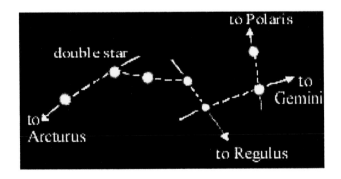

Figure 9 – Big Dipper as a sky benchmark

Juvenile Golden Eagle

Allegheny Front Hawk-watch spotters counted 163 Golden Eagles and 41 Bald Eagles (along with close to 8400 other raptors) following Somerset County's east ridge on their annual migration south in the autumn of 2001. See the **Appendix** for directions to the main watch site.

Week by week and day by day, the schedule of natural events is always changing. At any season of the year, there are exciting things to see and do outdoors in Somerset County, Pennsylvania. There is plenty of room to add some of your own favorite events or phenomena in the margins below.

January

➤ The constellation **Orion** is prominent in the night sky.
➤ Check conifer stands for birds like **Long-eared Owl** and **Northern Saw-whet Owl.**
➤ **Black bears** are having their cubs while denning.
➤ **Red foxes** are mating.
➤ **Lapland Longspurs, Snow Buntings,** and **Horned Larks** (all "snowbirds") visit manured fields.
➤ *Ice fishing* is possible in the stark cold of winter. High Point Lake is a favored spot.
➤ Many **bucks** have shed their antlers. Some retain them through the winter.
➤ Now is a good time to watch **oak** slabs crackle in the hearth. See it, hear it, feel it, smell it!
➤ Look for a bit of summer – **Eastern Bluebirds** and **Robins** are present *in small numbers* all winter long.

February

➤ **Great Horned Owls** are nesting on eggs, sometimes draped with snowfall.
➤ Many yard birds begin singing on sunny winter days.
➤ **Skunk cabbage** pushes up through the snow.
➤ Tapping of **sugar maple** trees begins for sap collection (~40 gallons sugar water = 1 gallon syrup).
➤ **Sallows, pinions,** and other **moths** will fly on warm (relatively!) nights. They like maple keelers.
➤ The earliest **mourning cloak** butterflies emerge in warmer years.
➤ **Red-winged Blackbirds** return in flocks.
➤ At the first real thaw, start checking shallow pools for **Jefferson's salamander** (earlier springs).
➤ **Walleye** begin to spawn when "ice out" occurs: sometimes in February, more often in March.

March (Spring!! – the most celebrated event in the natural year)

➤ **Wood frogs** begin calling: **spring peepers** are soon to follow.
➤ **Pussy willow** branches are in blossom. Bead fronds from last year's **sensitive ferns** are still in marshes.
➤ **Groundhogs** emerge from hibernation.
➤ Watch for the first **coltsfoot** along roadsides. Their flowers resemble those of dandelions.
➤ Check the big lakes for migrant **ducks, geese,** and **swans** as soon as the ice starts to melt.
➤ *Vernal Equinox* (equal time of night and day) occurs around the 20th . . . the start of spring is official.
➤ **Red-winged Blackbirds** are defending territories. **Meadowlarks** return.
➤ **Spotted salamanders** are breeding; any small pond in the country will do for a search – go at night.
➤ Cultivated yellow **forsythia** bushes begin to bloom all over the county.

April

➤ **Woodcocks** are "dancing" nightly.
➤ Hunt for **spring peepers** at night with a flashlight.
➤ **Hepatica, spring beauties, trailing arbutus, violets,** and **trillium** emerge. Hunting for **ramps** begins.
➤ **Barn Swallows** arrive mid-month. Their return brightens chore time.
➤ **Morel** collecting begins by mushroom hunters. **Black morels** are usually the first to emerge.
➤ The **earliest warblers** return: **Yellow-rumped Warbler** likely first among them.
➤ **Deer antlers** begin to develop.
➤ **Groundhog** chucklings are born.
➤ **Snakes** are now on the prowl.
➤ **Sarvis** is in bloom. It's also known as **serviceberry** or **Juneberry.**

May

- ➤ **Ruby-throated Hummingbirds** are here. **Orioles, tanagers,** and **Rose-breasted Grosbeaks** join them.
- ➤ **Flowering dogwood** is in bloom as it hails in the days of warm. Wild **azaleas** bloom in concert.
- ➤ **Lady slipper, Greek valerian, golden ragwort, bluets, Jack-in-the-pulpit,** (and *many* others) bloom.
- ➤ **Timber rattlesnakes** emerge from dens (when the oak leaves are the size of squirrel's ears).
- ➤ Green **spittlebug** nymphs, cloaked in their spittle, are numerous in hayfields (but mature by late June).
- ➤ **May beetles** ("June bugs") come to your screen door at night.
- ➤ **Warblers** are at peak migration around mid-month.
- ➤ **Bass** begin to spawn when water temperatures rise and remain above the 60 degree mark.
- ➤ **Sweet vernal grass, lilacs,** and **honeysuckle** grace the breeze.
- ➤ Look for migrant **shorebirds** wherever there is lots of mud or shallow water.
- ➤ **Crab apple** (or **hawthorn**) **trees** bloom mid to late month.

June

- ➤ Nesting birds are in full song early in the mornings. **Spring peepers** have largely grown silent.
- ➤ **Luna moths** near end of spring flight – check pole lights in the countryside.
- ➤ **Choke cherry** trees are in bloom.
- ➤ Most **fawns** are born this month: or late in May.
- ➤ Variety and numbers of **butterfly** species begin to grow.
- ➤ Look for **Osprey** on the nesting platforms at Lake Somerset and Cranberry Glade Lake.
- ➤ **Mountain laurel** is in full bloom by mid-month.
- ➤ **Snapping turtles** lay their eggs.
- ➤ *Summer Solstice* occurs around the 21st: summer's start is official and daylight time begins to decrease.
- ➤ **Fireflies** peak in the night meadows. **Spittlebug** nymphs molt into adults.

July

- ➤ Start picking **raspberries** and **blueberries.**
- ➤ **Rhododendron** blooms now in place of mountain laurel; also, the **milkweeds** bloom.
- ➤ **Shorebirds** start to appear as they migrate south. **Yellow Warblers** are hard to find after July.
- ➤ These are good nights for leisurely star observation.
- ➤ **Wooly mullein** dots all the country roadsides like miniature saguaro cacti.
- ➤ This is summer in all its glory. Go fishing!
- ➤ **Bluegill** spawn through much of the summer.
- ➤ **Early goldenrod,** the first of many species, comes into bloom. Sometimes it even flowers in late June.
- ➤ The rare **purple fringeless orchid** may be found in moist areas in late July and early August.
- ➤ **Monarch** caterpillars and chrysalises may be looked for. They're more common next month.
- ➤ **Black-and-yellow garden spiders** start to spin their large webs. Their numbers will increase.

August

- ➤ Wet weather brings the largest variety of **mushrooms.**
- ➤ **Katydids** begin their loud, night chorus and continue through September.
- ➤ **Red-spotted purple** butterflies are very numerous. August is the best time for **underwing moths.**
- ➤ **Perseid meteor shower** is the nighttime fireworks display around August 11-13 (12th is usually best).
- ➤ **Jewelweed** seed pods "explode" to the touch, and continue through September.
- ➤ **Wild blackberries** are ready to harvest.
- ➤ **Cardinal flower** blooms mid-month in moist areas and continues to early September.
- ➤ **Asters** are beginning to reach full bloom. Early ones appear at the start of the month.
- ➤ **Deerflies** are fading away! **Ironweed** and **Joe-pye-weed** make the wetlands purple and pink.
- ➤ **Nighthawk** migration signals summer's end; **Barn Swallows** depart the barns.
- ➤ Many **sedges** and **rushes** are fruiting and so may now be more easily identified.

September

- Hawk watchers begin observing the **raptor migration** at Allegheny Front outside of Central City.
- Scents of **goldenrod** and **Queen-Anne's-lace** are heavy on the fields. **Elderberries** are ripe.
- Passerine bird migration is in full sway; learn those fall warblers!
- **Asters** peak this month. **Ladies'-tresses** (orchids) and **gentians** bloom early to mid month.
- **Bald-faced hornet** nests appear, like big gray basketballs, in trees or building eaves.
- **Banded garden spiders** join the closely related **black-and-yellow garden spiders** in the meadows.
- **Daddy longlegs** are more common in autumn.
- **Monarch butterflies** begin to depart for destinations South.
- *Autmnal Equinox* (equal time of night and day) is around the 21st; fall officially begins.
- Some trees begin turning colorful. **Acorns** are falling.
- **Snakes** are gathering to den for the winter.

October

- First killing *frost* occurs any time this month.
- **Tawny cottongrass** (a sedge) waves its cotton in wetlands and bogs.
- **"Sheep's head"** or **hen-of-the-woods** mushrooms appear and are harvested for the pot.
- **Wooly-bear caterpillars** hit full stride. Look for "Halloween spiders" (orange **marbled orbweavers**).
- The 2nd weekend Of October is the usual peak of *fall foliage* colors.
- **Blackbirds** flock, and **Dark-eyed Juncos** begin to appear at feeders.
- **Witch hazel** starts to bloom even as its leaves are beginning to turn and fall.
- The constellation **Orion** is visible in the early morning hours.
- **Quaking aspen** leaves turn yellow after most other trees' leaves are down.
- **Bat** species that don't migrate south enter hibernaculums.
- **Ducks, geese, and swans** start coming through in large numbers (late in the month).

November

- **Milkweed pods** have opened and are releasing seeds.
- The last **dragonflies** are still flying in some years.
- **Golden Eagles** reach their peak of migration during early November (or late October) on Shaffer Ridge.
- Some **daisies, Queen-Anne's-lace,** and **chicory** still bloom early in the month.
- **Brook trout** have been spawning from late September through November.
- **Larch** trees glow with gold needles. **Common winterberry holly** (red berries) is now easy to see.
- Occasional turtles or snakes may still bask on warm days – most herps are hibernating by now.
- **Cut-leaved grape ferns** still dot the woodland floor here and there.
- The last **goldenrods** and **asters** fade by month's end.
- Watch for **Fox Sparrows** and **Yellow-bellied Sapsuckers** to migrate through the area.
- Late month is the peak of **white-tailed deer** rut.

December

- The "white rain" of the American Indians begins, or has begun, to fall.
- **Winter finches** may appear (**Evening Grosbeak, Redpoll, crossbills** *et al*) – keep your feeders filled.
- Now is a good time to test winter tree identification and mammal tracking skills.
- **Geminid meteor shower** on the 13th is on par with Perseids, but must be hardy to be outside and enjoy!
- **Christmas fern** and **ground pine** are collected for holiday greenery.
- Hurrah! Length of daylight begins to increase again. *Winter Solstice* is near the 21st and winter begins.
- **Great Horned Owls** are vocal and often heard from dusk to dawn.
- *Christmas Bird Counts* (CBCs) are held in late December or early January.
- A small percentage of **weasels** and **snowshoe hares** may turn white if winter is steady and cold.

Quotes of Note

Richard Adams:
Nature is not a competition. It doesn't really matter, when you go out, if you don't identify anything. What matters is the feeling heart.

Walt Whitman:
You must not know too much, or be too precise or scientific about birds and trees and flowers. A certain free margin . . . helps your enjoyment of these things.

Hans Dossenbach:
The greater the efforts we make to fathom the secrets of the birds, the more our knowledge expands, the clearer becomes our realization that the secrets of the birds will remain mysteries of nature as long as she abounds with the miracles of life.

Robert Frost:
Nature is always hinting at us. It hints over and over again. And suddenly we take the hint.

Ansel Adams:
I know of no sculpture, painting or music that exceeds the compelling spiritual command of the soaring shape of granite cliff and dome, of patina of light on rock and forest, and of the thunder and whispering of the falling, flowing waters.

John Burroughs:
I go to Nature to be soothed and healed, and to have my senses put in tune once more.

Cecil Frances Alexander:
All things bright and beautiful,
 All creatures great and small,
All things wise and wonderful,
 The Lord God made them all.

Edward Everett Hale: his pledge to the Lend-a-Hand Society
I am only one,
But still I am one.
I cannot do everything,
But still I can do something;
And because I cannot do everything,
I will not refuse to do the something that
I can do.

Ferris Bueller: (from the motion picture "Ferris Bueller's Day Off")
Life moves pretty fast. You don't stop and look around once in a while, you could miss it.

GEOLOGY & SOILS of Somerset County, PA

1. Mt. Davis – highest point in PA

2. Soil – where it begins

3. The Laurel Highlands

4. Low-volatility Bituminous Coal

5. Laurel Hill Sandstone Outcrop

MUSHROOMS & FUNGI of Somerset County, PA

6. Jack O'Lantern

7. Bear's Head Tooth

8. Bitter Bolete

WILDFLOWERS of Somerset County, PA

86. Jack-in-the-Pulpit

87. Trout-Lily

88. Pink Lady's-Slipper – white

89. Bloodroot

90. Red Trillium

91. White Trillium

92. Red Trillium – white form

WILDFLOWERS of Somerset County, PA

93. Coltsfoot

94. Round-lobed Hepatica

95. Marsh-Marigold

96. Bluets

97. Wild Ginger

98. Common Evening Primrose

99. Red Clover

100. Rabbit's-Foot Clover

WILDFLOWERS of Somerset County, PA

101. May Apple

102. Black Cohosh

103. Butter-and-Eggs

104. Indian-Pipe

105. Common Dandelion

106. Common Milkweed

107. Butterfly-Weed

108. Swamp Milkweed

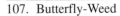

WILDFLOWERS of Somerset County, PA

109. Bee-Balm

110. Boneset

111. Black-eyed Susan

112. Common Cattail

113. Sneezeweed

114. American Bur Reed

115. Ox-Eye Daisy

116. Queen Anne's Lace

INSECTS of Somerset County, PA

194. Meadow Spittlebug – nymph

195. Green Lacewing

196. Red-legged Locust

197. Multicol. Asian Lady Beetle

198. Grapevine Beetle

199. Locust Borer

200. Six-spotted Green Tiger Beetle

201. Milkweed Beetle

202. Pennsylvania Firefly

203. Honey Bee

204. Giant Hornet

205. Common Water Strider

INSECTS of Somerset County, PA

206. Eastern Dobsonfly

207. Bald-Faced Hornet

208. Large Diving Beetle

209. Green Stink Bug

210. Green Stink Bug – nymph

INSECTS of Somerset County, PA

211. Fork-Tailed Bush Katydid

212. Carolina Locust

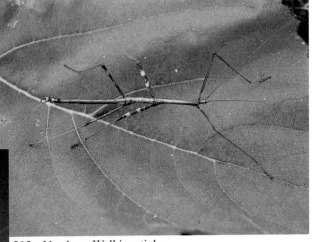

213. Northern Walkingstick

214. Praying Mantis

215. Praying Mantis – brown form

216. Question Mark – fall form

217. Black Swallowtail – male

218. Pearl Crescent

219. Red-spotted Purple

220. Mourning Cloak

221. Aphrodite Fritillary

222. Great Spangled Fritillary

BUTTERFLIES & MOTHS of Somerset County, PA

223. Red Admiral

224. Painted Lady

225. Tiger Swallowtail

226. Black Swallowtail caterpillar

227. Monarch – female

228. Monarch – male

229. Viceroy

230. Monarch caterpillar

BUTTERFLIES & MOTHS of Somerset County, PA

231. Monarch chrysalis

232. Baltimore

233. Eastern Tailed Blue

234. Hobomok Skipper

235. European Skipper

236. Alfalfa Butterfly – white

237. False Crocus Geometer

238. Beautiful Wood-Nymph

239. Bent-line Gray

240. The Green Marvel

241. Hickory Tussock Moth

242. Spotted Apatelodes

243. Promethea – female

244. Polyphemus

245. Yellow-banded Underwing

246. White Underwing

247. Polyphemus caterpillar

248. Luna – summer flight

249. Luna – spring flight

250. Cecropia

251. Io Moth – male

252. Rosy Maple Moth

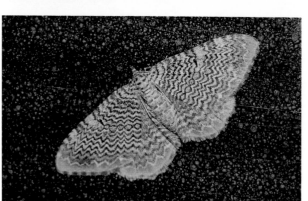

253. Ferguson's Scallop Shell

254. Clymene Moth

BUTTERFLIES & MOTHS of Somerset County, PA

255. The Neighbor

256. Confused Haploa

257. Dogwood Thyatirid

258. Common Lytrosis

259. Lettered Habrosyne

260. Large Tolype

261. Waved Sphinx

262. Hog Sphinx

263. "Wooly-Bear"

264. Rose Hooktip

265. Arched Hooktip

266. Pepper-and-Salt Geometer –
melanic

267. Virgin Tiger Moth

268. Giant Leopard Moth

269. Hummingbird Moth

270. Tulip-Tree Beauty

271. Brown-hooded Owlet caterpillar

FISHES of Somerset County, PA

272. Brook Trout

273. Northern Pike

274. White Sucker

275. Mottled Sculpin

FISHES of Somerset County, PA

276. Bullhead & young Channel Catfish

277. Pumpkinseed

278. Largemouth Bass

279. Banded Killfish

FISHES of Somerset County, PA

280. Creek Chubs – immature

281. Golden Shiner

282. Johnny Darter

283. Yellow Perch

AMPHIBIANS of Somerset County, PA

284. Northern Spring Peeper

285. Mountain Chorus Frog

286. Pickerel Frog

287. Wood Frog

288. American Toad

AMPHIBIANS of Somerset County, PA

289. Green Frog – female

290. Green Frog – male

291. Green Frog tadpole

292. Bullfrog (two – look close!)

293. Red-spotted Newt

294. Red Eft

AMPHIBIANS of Somerset County, PA

295. Jefferson Salamander

296. Spotted Salamander

297. Long-tailed Salamander

298. Mountain Dusky Salamander

299. Slimy Salamander

300. Red-backed Salamander

REPTILES of Somerset County, PA

301. Eastern Smooth Green Snake

302. Black Rat Snake

303. Northern Redbelly Snake

304. Northern Brown Snake

305. Northern Ringneck Snake

306. Eastern Garter Snake

REPTILES of Somerset County, PA

307. Northern Water Snake

309. Northern Copperhead

311. Timber Rattlesnake – yellow phase

308. Eastern Milk Snake

310. Timber Rattlesnake – black phase

REPTILES of Somerset County, PA

312. Queen Snake

313. Wood Turtle

314. Midland Painted Turtle

315. Eastern Box Turtle – male

316. Common Snapping Turtle

BIRDS of Somerset County, PA

317. Canada Geese and goslings

318. Yellow-billed Cuckoo

319. Blue Jay

320. Rose-breasted Grosbeak

321. Great Egret – PA endangered

BIRDS of Somerset County, PA

322. Turkey Vulture

323. Ring-necked Pheasant

324. Ruffed Grouse

325. Baird's Sandpiper

326. Western Sandpiper

327. Ring-billed Gull

328. Ruby-throated Hummingbird

329. Northern Flicker

330. Black-capped Chickadee

331. Yellow-rumped Warbler

332. Song Sparrow

333. Cardinal

BIRDS of Somerset County, PA

334. Long-eared Owl

335. Barn Swallow

336. Eastern Kingbird

337. Common Loon – winter

338. Mallard hen and drake

339. Red-tailed Hawk

340. Eastern Screech-Owl – red fledgling

BIRDS of Somerset County, PA

341. Great Blue Heron rookery

342. American Goldfinch

343. Wild Turkey

344. Virginia Opossum

345. Groundhog

346. Deer Mouse

347. Meadow Jumping Mouse

348. Red Squirrel

349. Small-footed Myotis

MAMMALS of Somerset County, PA

350. Little Brown Myotis

351. Indiana Myotis hibernating
above the turnpike tunnel –
a federally endangered species

352. Raccoon

353. White-tailed Deer – fawn

354. White-tailed Deer – buck

MAMMALS of Somerset County, PA

355. Eastern Chipmunk

356. Eastern Cottontail

357. Red Fox

358. Southern Flying Squirrel

359. Black Bear cub & author

360. My favorite mammals: Andrew, Jill, James, & Nicholas

ADDITIONAL SPECIES of Somerset County, PA

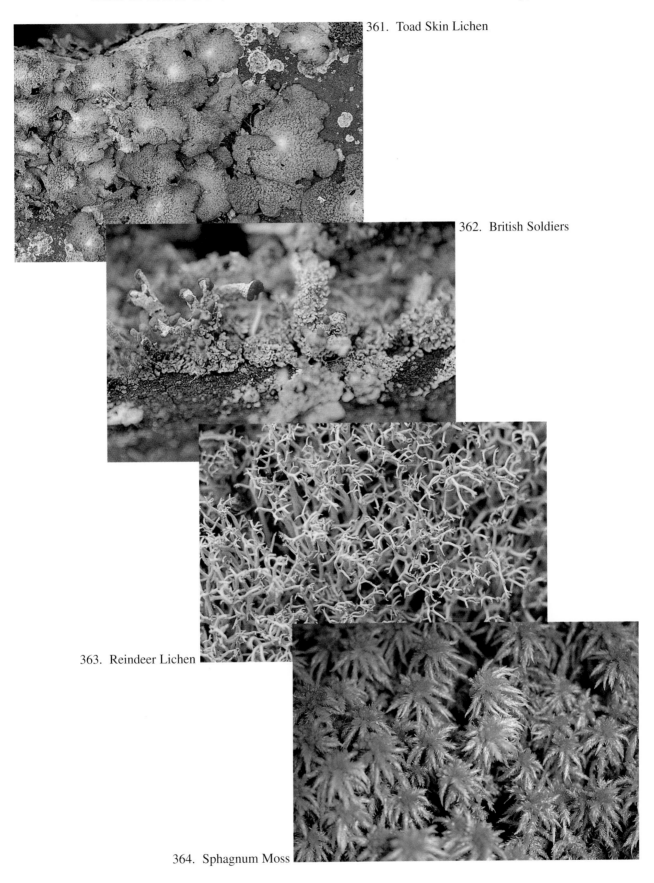

361. Toad Skin Lichen

362. British Soldiers

363. Reindeer Lichen

364. Sphagnum Moss

ADDITIONAL SPECIES of Somerset County, PA

365. Pond Papershell

366. Snail – *Mesodon thyroidus*

367. Common Scutigera

368. Crayfish – *Oronectes obscurus*

THE SKIES ABOVE US of Somerset County, PA

369. Venus & Crescent Moon

370. Northern Lights over Stoystown

371. Mackerel Sky

372. Our star, the Sun

373. The Moon

THE SKIES ABOVE US of Somerset County, PA

374. Cumulus

375. Cirrus

376. Thunderheads – Cumulonimbus

377. Stratus – "Red in the morning…"

SOMERSET COUNTRY SCENERY

378. Black & Gold

379. Autumn Dairy Farm

380. Spring Green Returns

381. Field of Webs

382. Pink Sunset

383. Frosty Winter Trees

SOMERSET COUNTRY SCENERY

384. Coal Run Falls

385. Ironweed Meadow

386. Autumn Red Maple

387. Snowfall by Mountain Stream